**Cultural and
Geographical
Exploration**

Lighthouses: Beacons of the Sea

CHRONICLES FROM *NATIONAL GEOGRAPHIC*

Cultural and Geographical Exploration

Cultural and Geographical Exploration

Lighthouses: Beacons of the Sea

CHRONICLES FROM *NATIONAL GEOGRAPHIC*

Arthur M. Schlesinger, jr.
Senior Consulting Editor

Fred L. Israel
General Editor

CHELSEA HOUSE PUBLISHERS

Philadelphia

CHELSEA HOUSE PUBLISHERS

Editor in Chief Stephen Reginald
Managing Editor James D. Gallagher
Production Manager Pamela Loos
Art Director Sara Davis
Director of Photography Judy L. Hasday
Senior Production Editor LeeAnne Gelletly

The Chelsea House World Wide Web site address is
http://www.chelseahouse.com

First Printing

1 3 5 7 9 8 6 4 2

Library of Congress Cataloging-in-Publication Data

Lighthouses : beacons of the sea / text provided by National Geographic Society.
p.   cm. – (Cultural and geographical exploration)
Text originally published in National geographic.
Includes index.
Summary: Text originally published in "National Geographic" describes the lighthouse
system around the coasts of the United States, from the eighteenth century to the
early years of the twentieth century.
ISBN 0-7910-5444-6 (hc)
1. Lighthouses—United States Juvenile literature.
[1. Lighthouses—History.]   I. National Goegraphic Society (U.S.)
II. National geographic.   III. Series.
VK1023.L5323   1999
387.1'55—dc21   99-26494
                                                      CIP

CONTENTS

"THE GREATEST EDUCATIONAL JOURNAL"

When the first *National Geographic* magazine appeared in October 1888, the United States totaled 38 states. Grover Cleveland was President. The nation's population hovered around 60 million. Great Britain's Queen Victoria also ruled as the Empress of India. William II became Kaiser of Germany that year. Czar Alexander III ruled Russia, and the Turkish Empire stretched from the Balkans to the tip of Arabia. To Westerners, the Far East was still a remote and mysterious land. Throughout the world, riding the back of an animal was the principal means of transportation. Unexplored and unmarked places dotted the global map.

On January 13, 1888, thirty-three men—scientists, cartographers, inventors, scholars, and explorers—met in Washington, D.C. They had accepted an invitation from Gardiner Greene Hubbard (1822–1897), the first president of the Bell Telephone Company and a leader in the education of the deaf, to form the National Geographic Society "to increase and diffuse geographic knowledge." One of the assembled group noted that they were the "first explorers of the Grand Canyon and the Yellowstone, those who had carried the American flag farthest north, who had measured the altitude of our famous mountains, traced the windings of our coasts and rivers, determined the distribution of flora and fauna, enlightened us in the customs of the aborigines, and marked out the path of storm and flood." Nine months later, the first issue of *National Geographic* magazine was sent out to 165 charter members. Today, more than a century later, membership has grown to an astounding 11 million in more than 170 nations. Several times that number regularly read the monthly issues of the *National Geographic* magazine.

The first years were difficult ones for the new magazine. The earliest volumes seem dreadfully scientific and quite dull. The articles in Volume I, No. 1 set the tone—W. M. Davis, "Geographic Methods in Geologic Investigation," followed by W. J. McGee, "The Classification of Geographic Forms by Genesis." Issues came out erratically—three in 1889, five in 1890, four in 1891, and two in 1895. In January 1896 "an illustrated monthly" was added to the title. The November issue that year contained a photograph of a half-naked Zulu bride and bridegroom in their wedding finery staring full face into the camera. But, a reader must have wondered what to make of the accompanying text: "These people . . . possess some excellent traits, but are horribly cruel when once they have smelled blood." In hopes of expanding circulation, the Board of Managers offered newsstand copies at $.25 each and began to accept advertising. But the magazine essentially remained unchanged. Circulation rose only slightly.

In January 1898, shortly after Gardiner Greene Hubbard's death, his son-in-law Alexander Graham Bell (1847–1922) agreed to succeed him as the second president of the National Geographic Society. Bell invented the telephone in 1876 and, while pursuing his lifelong goal of improving the lot of the deaf, had turned his amazingly versatile mind to contemplating such varied problems as human flight, air conditioning, and popularizing geography. The society then had about 1,100 members—the magazine was on the edge of bankruptcy. Bell did not want the job. He wrote in his diary, though, that he accepted leadership of the society "in order to save it." "Geography is a fascinating subject and it can be made interesting," he told the board of directors. Bell abandoned the unsuccessful attempt to increase circulation through newsstand sales. "Our journal," he wrote, "should go to members, people who believe in our work and want to help." He understood that the lure for prospective members should be an association with a society that made it possible for the average person to share with kings and scientists the excitement of sending an expedition to a strange land or an explorer to an inaccessible region. This idea, more than any other, has been responsible for the growth of the National Geographic Society and for the popularity of the magazine. "I can well remember," recalled Bell in 1912, "how the idea was laughed at that we should ever reach a membership of ten thousand." That year it had soared to 107,000!

Bell attributed this phenomenal growth, though, to one man who had transformed the *National Geographic* magazine into "the greatest educational journal in the world"—Gilbert H. Grosvenor (1875–1966). Bell had hired Grosvenor, then 24, in 1899 as the National Geographic Society's first full-time employee, "to put some life into the magazine." He personally escorted the new editor, who would become his son-in-law, to the society's headquarters—a small rented room shared with the American Forestry Association on the fifth floor of a building near the U.S. Treasury in downtown Washington. Grosvenor remembered the headquarters "littered with old magazines, newspapers, and a few record books and six enormous boxes crammed with *Geographics* returned by the newsstands." "No desk!" exclaimed Bell. "I'll send you mine." That afternoon, delivery men brought Grosvenor a large walnut rolltop and the new editor began to implement Bell's instructions—to transform the magazine from one of cold geographic fact "expressed in hieroglyphic terms which the layman could not understand into a vehicle for carrying the living, breathing, human-interest truth about this great world of ours to the people." And what did Bell consider appropriate "geographic subjects"? He replied: "The world and all that is in it is our theme."

Grosvenor shared Bell's vision of a great society and magazine that would disseminate geographic knowledge. "I thought of geography in terms of its Greek root: *geographia*—a description of the world," he later wrote. "It thus becomes the most catholic of subjects, universal in appeal, and embracing nations, people, plants, birds, fish. We would never lack interesting subjects." To attract readers, Grosvenor had to change the public attitude toward geography, which he knew was regarded as "one of the dullest of all subjects, something to inflict upon schoolboys and avoid in later life." He wondered why certain books that relied heavily on geographic description remained popular—Charles Darwin's *Voyage of the Beagle*, Richard Dana Jr.'s *Two Years Before the Mast*, and even Herodotus's *History*. Why did readers for generations—and with Herodotus's travels, for 20 centuries—return to these books? What did these volumes, which used so many geographic descriptions, have in common? What was the secret? According to Grosvenor, the answer was that "each was an accurate, eyewitness, firsthand account. Each contained simple straightforward writing—writing that sought to make pictures in the reader's mind."

Gilbert Grosvenor was editor of the *National Geographic* magazine for 55 years, from 1899 until 1954. Each of the 660 issues under his direction had been a highly readable geography textbook. He took Bell's vision and made it a reality. Acclaimed as "Mr. Geography," he discovered the earth anew for himself and for millions around the globe. He charted the dynamic course that the National Geographic Society and its magazine followed for more than half a century. In so doing, he forged an instrument for world education and understanding unique in this or any age. Under his direction, the *National Geographic* magazine grew in circulation from a few hundred copies—he recalled carrying them to the post office on his back—to more than five million at the time of his retirement as editor, enough for a stack 25 miles high.

This Chelsea House series celebrates Grosvenor's first 25 years as editor of the *National Geographic*. "The mind must see before it can believe," said Grosvenor. From the earliest days, he filled the magazine with photographs and established another Geographic principle—to portray people in their natural attire or lack of it. Within his own editorial committee, young Grosvenor encountered the prejudice that photographs had to be "scientific." Too often, this meant dullness. To Grosvenor, every picture and sentence had to be interesting to the layperson. "How could you educate and inform if you lost your audience by boring your readers?" Grosvenor would ask his staff. He persisted and succeeded in making the *National Geographic* magazine reflect this fascinating world.

To the young-in-heart of every age there is magic in the name *National Geographic*. The very words conjure up enchanting images of faraway places, explorers and scientists, sparkling seas and dazzling mountain peaks, strange plants, animals, people, and customs. The small society founded in 1888 "for the increase and diffusion of geographic knowledge" grew, under the guidance of one man, to become a great force for knowledge and understanding. This achievement lies in the genius of Gilbert H. Grosvenor, the architect and master builder of the National Geographic Society and its magazine.

Fred L. Israel
The City College of the City University of New York

LIGHTHOUSES

Fred L. Israel

John Oliver La Gorce (1879–1959) served as president of the National Geographic Society (1954–57) and editor of the magazine (1954–57), succeeding Gilbert H. Grosvenor in both positions. La Gorce was associated with the National Geographic for 54 years.

Grosvenor hired 25-year old "Jack" La Gorce as an assistant secretary in 1905. In that year, membership had increased from 3,256 to 11,479—a gain of 253 percent. The additional revenue enabled Grosvenor to advise his father-in-law, Alexander Graham Bell, that he could discontinue his annual contribution of $1,200. The increased revenue also provided the $75 a month for the new assistant. When La Gorce died, the National Geographic Society, the nonprofit organization to which he devoted his great talents and energy, had some 1,000 employees and a world-wide membership of 2,500,000.

In recognition of La Gorce's distinguished contribution to writing and the study of geography, a mountain and a glacier in Alaska were named for him. La Gorce Arch, a fantastic rock formation in Utah, bears his name. In Antarctica, there are the La Gorce Mountains and the La Gorce Peak. When Admiral Richard Byrd led his first South Polar expedition in 1928–30, he set up the La Gorce Meteorological Station. On Byrd's 1933 return trip, he appointed La Gorce honorary postmaster of Little America at Antarctica.

La Gorce wrote 15 articles for the *National Geographic* on subjects as diverse as Puerto Rico, Pennsylvania, aquariums, and Romania. Others dealt with fishing, his favorite sport. He personally edited all editions of the society's comprehensive *Book of Fishes*.

In the fall of 1914, La Gorce was on the first cruise ship to pass through the Panama Canal from New York to San Francisco. His first article for the *National Geographic*, the idea of which came during this trip, dealt with the coastline of the southeastern United States from the Virginia capes to the Rio Grande, the "battleground of nature." Most of the splendid photographs were taken by H.C. Mann, who then ranked as one of the foremost photographic artists in the country. La Gorce continued his study of the Atlantic seacoast in a June 1918 article. We include two essays in this compilation as a tribute and remembrance of John Oliver La Gorce, an outstanding geographer who guided both the National Geographic Society and magazine for so many years.

Complementing the La Gorce essays is a wonderful history of coastal lighthouses by George R. Putnam, who contributed six articles to the National Geographic between 1897 and 1936 on maritime guides for shipping. Together these three articles attempt to define the precarious border between land and sea. Putnam deals with lighthouses, those legendary monuments that have captured the imagination of artists and poets for ages. These structures have perched on treacherous coasts, their lights serving as guiding beacons for sailors, from the ancient world forward.

The very first lighthouses were undoubtedly volcanoes, since their glow was visible both day and night. Early mariners also relied on bonfires along the shoreline. Then, sometime during the third century B.C., it was realized that elevated fires could be seen from greater distances than fires burning on the beach. Hence, the idea developed of building tall stone towers on whose tops fires would be burned. And with this began a legacy of one of the most important and fascinating structures in maritime history—the coastal lighthouse. Today, these structures serve chiefly as a reminder of a time past, a time before radar, sonar, and onboard electronics. Until recently, though, lighthouses were the principal aids for safe navigation.

Vol. XXIV, No. 1   WASHINGTON   January, 1913

BEACONS OF THE SEA
Lighting the Coasts of the United States

By George R. Putnam, Commissioner of Lighthouses

THE sea-coast line under the jurisdiction of the United States is 48,881 statute miles, measured in three-mile steps. The general government provides lighthouses and other aids to navigation along all this coast, with the exception of the Philippine Islands, 11,511 miles, and Panama, where the marking of the coasts is maintained by the local governments. In addition, the United States provides lights along the American shores of the Great Lakes, 4,020 miles, and on interior and coastal rivers, 5,478 miles.

The United States Lighthouse Service thus maintains lights and other aids to navigation along 46,828 miles of coastline and river channels, a length equal to nearly twice the circumference of the earth. In this distance *it has 12,824 aids to navigation of all classes, sufficient to place one every two miles around the equator.*

In respect to territory covered and aids maintained, it is much the most extensive service of its kind under a single management. There are 1,462 lights above the order of river-post lights, and there are 762 lights having resident keepers, 51 light-vessel stations, and 438 lighted buoys. The total lighted aids of all kinds is 4,516. There are in all 933 fog signals, of which 510 are fog-signal stations, 43 submarine bells, 124 whistling buoys, and 256 bell buoys. There are 6,281 unlighted buoys, and 1,474 daymarks, or unlighted beacons. There are also 516 private aids to navigation, maintained at private expense, but under government supervision.

This service is carried on through an organization of 19 districts, under a central office in Washington. Each district is in charge of a lighthouse inspector and has a local office and one or more supply depots and lighthouse tenders. In all, there are 46 of these small vessels which carry the supplies to the stations and place and maintain the buoys and light vessels.

About 5,500 men are required for the lighthouse work, of whom 211 are in the executive, engineering, and clerical force, 1,733 are keepers of lights and depots, 1,570 care for post lights, 1,516 are on vessels, and 489 are in the construction and repair force.

The entire personnel is under the civil-service rules, and appointments and promotions are on a strictly merit system. This is of great importance for the maintenance of good

THE GENERAL LIGHTHOUSE DEPOT ON STATEN ISLAND, NEW YORK HARBOR

Lighthouse vessels are here repaired, buoys and supplies purchased, and special apparatus made and tested. Note the variety of gas buoys and other buoys on the dock, and light-ships and tenders in the basin.

organization and rigid discipline in a purely technical service on the efficient conduct of which is directly dependent the safety of all the lives and all the property carried on the seas and the navigable waters of this country.

The annual maintenance cost of the entire service is close to $5,000,000, and in addition in recent years there has been expended about $1,000,000 a year on new lighthouse works and vessels. This service is supported by appropriations out of the general revenues, and no special light taxes are collected from shipping, as is customary in other countries.

At all important light stations there are from two to five keepers, who maintain a continuous watch of the light at night and of the approach of fog at all times. At less important stations there is but one keeper, or sometimes a single keeper cares for several neighboring lights. The average pay of keepers is less than $600 per year, but they receive also a ration allowance and usually quarters and fuel. The maximum salary at difficult offshore stations is $1,008. For the care of a post light along the rivers about $10 a month is paid, but this requires only a small amount of work each day.

At the general lighthouse depot on Staten Island, New York harbor, shops are maintained for the repair and manufacture of special lighthouse apparatus. This is also a general supply station for the service, supplies and equipment being purchased and tested and experimental and designing work being carried on. Many of the lighthouse vessels are overhauled or outfitted here. There are employed in this depot and offices 253 persons.

Light stations and vessels are inspected four times a year, and the districts and offices are themselves inspected from time to time by a general inspector and a traveling auditor.

An accurate cost keeping system has recently been introduced for the entire lighthouse service, so that at the end of the year the principal items of cost for each feature can readily be ascertained and compared. The following are average annual costs of operating various features of the service: Large lighthouse tender, $40,500; light vessel on exposed station, $15,300; important light station, with fog signal, $4,200; same without fog signal, $3,000; river-post light, $90; gas buoy, $100 to $300, according to size and type.

FAITHFUL LIGHT-KEEPERS

Although the pay is small and the life often lonely, the work attracts as a rule an excellent class of faithful men, willing to take large risks in doing their duty and also in helping those in distress. There are many cases of faithful service and bravery, of which the following are a few instances:

The hurricane of September, 1906, did serious damage to lighthouse property along the Gulf coast and a number of lives were lost at Sand Island and at Horn Island light stations; at the latter the keeper, his wife, and daughter being drowned. Twenty-three lights were destroyed by this storm. On October 3 the inspector of the eighth district made this report: "The employees of the Lighthouse Service have, as was to be expected, maintained its credit. I have heard stories of gallant actions, and I have witnessed the uncomplaining manner in which they and their families have taken their great losses and deprivations, also their cheerfulness in beginning all over again."

The keeper of post lights on the St. Johns River, Florida, after being severely injured, went on with his work, as he tells in this report, in May, 1912: "I arrived at the light at 9:30 a.m. I took the lamp out, and as I went to blow it out it exploded and knocked me off the light (22 feet), and I did not know anything until 12 a.m. When I came to I found the lamp gone. I crawled back to the boat (250 feet) , got another lamp and put it on the beacon and lit it. Then came home (8 miles). Injury: broken leg just above the ankle and severe bruised shin and bruised arm and lick on head."

There is a pathetic story of the keeper of Key West light, who after 35 years of service became so absorbed in his duty that he would not leave his task, even for a short vacation, laboring under the delusion that no one but himself could properly care for the light. On a certain very stormy night a ship was wrecked near the fort at Key West. The keeper, then nearly 70 years of age, excited by the storm and the prolonged whistle blasts of the unfortunate vessel, insisted that the wreck was due to the front-range light being out, although it had just been examined by his son and found burning properly. In spite of his feeble condition he procured a lantern and, resisting efforts to detain him, went on foot in the storm to the range light and satisfied himself that it was really burning. He died not long afterward.

The keeper of Van Weis Point light, New York, died recently at the age of 93 years, having tended this light for 52 years.

At present there is no provision in this country for the retirement of light-keepers on account of age, long service, or disability resulting from their work.

The keeper of the most distant light in Alaska—Cape Sarichef—returned recently, his first absence in three years. At this station there is sometimes an interval of five months

THE PRESENT BOSTON LIGHT
Built in 1783 by Massachusetts and ceded to the United States in 1790 (see page 7).

between mails, and the keeper's only neighbor is a trapper, 10 miles away. A light-keeper on the Columbia River, Oregon, has taken only two days leave in 23 years, and one of these two days was for the purpose of being married.

WOMEN LIGHT-KEEPERS

There are a number of women light-keepers. One of these, the keeper of Angel Island light in San Francisco Bay, reported that after the machinery of the fog signal was disabled on July 2, 1906, she "had struck the bell by hand for 20 hours and 35 minutes, until the fog lifted," and that on July 4, when the machinery was further disabled, she "stood all night on the platform outside and struck the bell with a nail hammer with all my might. The fog was dense."

A widely known woman light-keeper was Ida Lewis, who died about a year ago. She lived at Lime Rock lighthouse, on a ledge in Newport harbor, for 57 years, her father having been appointed keeper when she was 12 years old. She was keeper of the light for 32 years. There are reports of her having rescued 13 persons from drowning. On one occasion, it is said, she saved three men who had swamped while attempting to pick up a sheep, and then she rescued the sheep also.

Because of the difficult life, keepers at isolated stations are granted shore liberty and leave 72 days a year, and crews of light vessels 90 days a year.

SANDY HOOK LIGHTHOUSE, NEW YORK

This and Cape Henlopen lighthouse, both built in 1764, are the oldest existing lighthouse towers in this country. The walls at the base are 7 feet thick.

THE BOSTON LIGHT WAS THE FIRST AMERICAN LIGHTHOUSE

The first lighthouse on this continent was built by the province of Massachusetts, in 1715-1716, on an island in the entrance to Boston harbor. In 1713 a committee reported to the General Court on "the most convenient Place for Erecting a Light House, which will be of great Use not only for the Preservation of the Lives and Estates of Persons designing for the Harbour of Boston and Charlestown but of any other Place within the Massachusetts Bay," and the court resolved "that the Projection will be of general publick Benefit and Service and is worthy to be encouraged," and that the want of such

a lighthouse "hath been a great Discouragement to Navigation by the loss of the lives and Estates of several of His Majesties Subjects."

In 1719 the keeper petitioned the General Court "that a great Gun be placed on Said Island to answer Ships in a Fog." The court voted the gun, and it was probably the earliest fog signal established in this country (see page 4).

The light was supported by light dues of one penny per ton, levied by the receiver of impost at Boston on all incoming and outgoing vessels except coasters. This lighthouse was an object of attack during the early part of the Revolutionary War, and was burned by the Americans and finally blown up by the British in 1776. A new lighthouse on the same site was

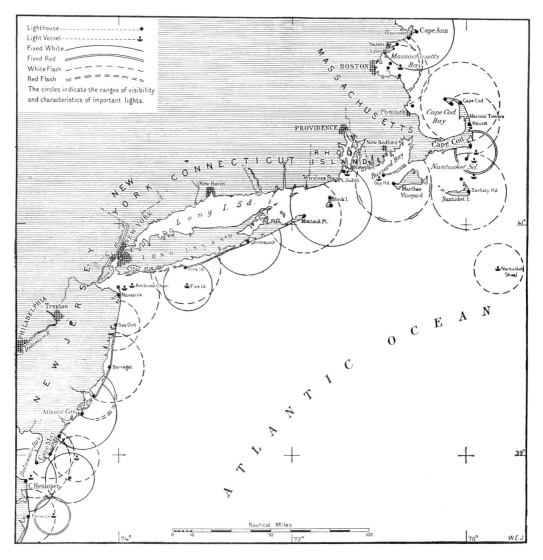

CHART SHOWING THE LIGHTS THAT MARK THE APPROACHES TO THE
GREAT HARBORS OF BOSTON, NEW YORK, AND PHILADELPHIA

Note the overlapping of the arcs of visibility of lights on an important coast. The lights differ in character and thus may easily be distinguished.

built in 1783 by Massachusetts, and this, with various alterations, is the present Boston light.

Although candles and even coal fires appear to have been used in lighthouse illumi-nation in England to a much later date, Boston light was probably illuminated from the first by oil lamps. In 1789 the light was produced by 16 lamps in groups of 4. Crude lenses and reflec-

AN ENDORSEMENT BY PRESIDENT WASHINGTON, IN HIS OWN HANDWRITING, ON A LIGHTHOUSE DOCUMENT

Showing the caution exercised by the first President in approving a contract for making a chain for a buoy (see page 10)

tors were fitted in 1811, and also revolving mechanism, it having previously been a fixed light. In 1838 Boston light was described as "a revolving light, consisting of 14 Argand lamps, with parabolic reflectors," the lamps being "of about the volume of similar lamps in family use." In 1839 large reflectors 21 inches in diameter were fitted to this light. Boston light was provided with a Fresnel lens in 1859.

Apparently the gun was the only fog signal at this station until about 1852, when a fog-bell was installed. A mechanical striking bell was installed in 1869, in 1872 a fog trumpet, and in 1887 an air siren.

THE ESTABLISHMENT OF OUR LIGHTHOUSE SERVICE WAS ONE OF THE FIRST ACTS OF THE FEDERAL GOVERNMENT

Several other lighthouses were built and maintained by the colonial governments. On the organization of the national government, at the first session of Congress, an act was passed, approved on August 7, 1789, providing that all expenses "in the necessary support, maintenance and repairs of all lighthouses, beacons, buoys and public piers erected, placed, or sunk before the passing of this act, at the entrance of, or within any bay, inlet, harbor, or port of the United States, for rendering the navigation thereof easy and safe, shall be defrayed out of the Treasury of the United States." Thus the Lighthouse Service was one of the earliest established by the Federal government, though it has been conducted under several different forms of administration.

The maintenance of lighthouses, buoys, and other navigational aids was, at the organization of the government, placed under the Treasury Department, and the details of lighthouse work were directed personally by the Secretary of the Treasury—Alexander Hamilton—by whom many of the earlier papers are signed. This work was during two later periods placed under the Commissioner of Revenue.

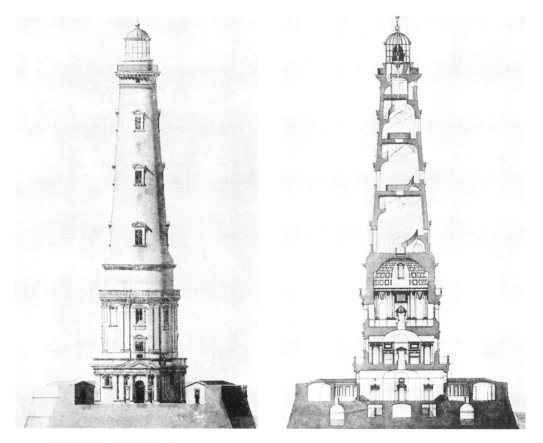

VIEW AND SECTION OF THE BEAUTIFUL LIGHTHOUSE ON THE COAST OF
FRANCE, PHARE DE CORDOUAN, COMPLETED IN 1611 AND SINCE ALTERED:
THE OLDEST SEA-SWEPT LIGHTHOUSE NOW IN EXISTENCE (SEE PAGE 20).

In 1820 the administration of the lighthouses devolved upon the Fifth Auditor of the Treasury, who was popularly known as the general superintendent of lights. Mr. Stephen Pleasonton discharged these duties for 32 years. In 1852 Congress established the United States Lighthouse Board, composed of three naval officers, three army engineers, and two civilians, with the Secretary of the Treasury as *ex-officio* President of the Board. The Chairmen of this Board were Admirals in the Navy, with the single exception of Prof. Joseph Henry, who was Chairman from 1871 to 1878. In 1910 the present Bureau of Lighthouses was established by Congress, under charge of a Commissioner of Lighthouses and other executive officers appointed by the President. The Lighthouse Service is now a part of the Department of Commerce and Labor, to which it was transferred from the Treasury in 1903.

I think the keepers of light-ses should be dismissed for small degrees of remissness, because of the calamities which even these pro-duce, & that the opinion of Col⁰. Newton in this case is of sufficient authority for the removal of the present keeper.

Th. Jefferson

Dec. 31. 01.

AN ENDORSEMENT BY PRESIDENT JEFFERSON IN HIS OWN HANDWRITING
Expressing his opinion of the responsibility of light-keepers (see page 16).

Under the act of 1789, 13 lighthouses were ceded to the United States by the several States, though apparently but eight of these were in actual operation at the date of the act (these are the eight first named in the list). The following are the lighthouses ceded, most of which are standing at the present time, although much altered:

Portsmouth Harbor, N.H.
Boston, Mass.
Plymouth (Gurnet), Mass.
Brant Point, Nantucket Island, Mass.
Beavertail, Newport, R.I.
Sandy Hook, N.Y.
Cape Henlopen, Del.
Charleston, S.C.
Portland Head, Maine.
Newburyport Harbor, Plum Id., Mass.
Cape Ann, Thatcher Island, Mass.
New London Harbor, Conn.
Tybee, Ga.

The oldest of the existing lighthouse structures in this country is the tower at Sandy Hook, New York, built in 1764. The lighthouse at Cape Henlopen, Delaware, was completed the same year. These are similar in design—massive structures of stone and brick, with walls 7 feet thick at the base (see page 5).

PERSONAL ATTENTION GIVEN BY PRESIDENT WASHINGTON TO LIGHTHOUSE MATTERS

Massachusetts, in ceding her lighthouses, showed her caution with respect to the new government by providing "that if the United States shall at any time hereafter neglect to keep lighted, and in repair, any one or more of the lighthouses aforesaid, that then the grant of such lighthouse or lighthouses so neglected shall be void and of no effect;" and also, "that if the United States shall at any time hereafter make any compensation to any one of the United States for the cession of any lighthouse ... like compensation be made to this Commonwealth by the United States, for the cession of the Light Houses aforesaid, in proportion to their respective values."

There are many interesting documents in the early archives of the service showing the attention given by high officers of the government to matters of lighthouse detail. President Washington personally approved such contracts as these: for the purchase of spermaceti oil for Cape Henry lighthouse, "to erect, sink, and build a well for water" for Cape Henlopen lighthouse, and for making "a mooring chain for one of the Floating Beacons of the Delaware Bay." On the last document appears the endorsement, all in Washington's handwriting, "April 27th, 1793, Approved, so far as it respects the new chain; but is there an entire loss of the old one? Gº. Washington." There is a proposal for Tybee lighthouse "for a hanging stair case for the sum of £160," or "should a plain square stair case be preferred,', for £110, with the endorsement, "Approved with the plain stair case. Gº. Washington."

During the earlier administrations the salaries of lighthouse-keepers were fixed by the President, and appointments of keepers were approved by him. The following document is of interest as showing the salaries then paid:

"UNITED STATES, *July 18th, 1793.*

"By the President's command T. Lear has the honor to inform the Secretary of the Treasury, that the President having duly considered the Representation of the Commissioner of the Revenue and the other documents relative to the compensations of the Keepers of the Light Houses, which were put into his hands by the Secretary, approves of the alterations of certain compensations as suggested by the Secretary, viz:

"1st. For the Keeper of the Light Houses on Thatcher's Island per annum, 266⅔ doll.

"2. do. Boston Bay, 266⅔ doll.

"3. do. Plymouth, 200 doll.

"4. do. Portland Head, 160 doll.

"5. do. Conanicut, 160 doll.

"6. do. New London, 120 doll.

"7. do. Sandy Hook, 266⅔ doll.

"To commence from the 1st day of the present Month.—

"The President thinks it proper that the Keeper of the Light House at Portsmouth be informed, that he must reside on the spot where the Light House is, if he continues in that office, and that he will not be permitted to employ a deputy to take care of the Light House, unless upon some special occasion.

TOBIAS LEAR,
"Secretary to the President of the United States."

The Commissioner of the Revenue in 1797 writes to the Secretary of the Treasury regarding salaries of keepers: "In the case of Major _____, there are the advantages of plenty of fuel, without expense, upon the public land, the opportunity to fish for his family use, or even for sale, a boat to fish in will be furnished

LANDING THE RELIEF AT THE EDDYSTONE
The keepers in turn are allowed shore liberty. It is often difficult to land at a wave-swept lighthouse.

for passing to the main, there is a little land for tillage and grass, and for a plentiful garden. The place is represented to be very healthy .... I have been thus particular because the salaries of keepers appear to have been subjected to some miscalculation on their parts from the unnecessary degree of former standing, which some of the candidates have had. It is plain at first view, that the above duties are not in their nature adapted to the standing of a field officer, or of a Major of Brigade."

A recommendation of a person for appointment as keeper in 1809 stated that the applicant "being by occupation a mason will engage to keep the Light House white washed, should he receive the appointment, free from any expense to the Government as long as he is its Keeper."

THE FOURTH AND PRESENT EDDYSTONE LIGHTHOUSE,
COMPLETED IN 1881 (SEE PAGE 20)

THE PETITIONS OF EBENEZER SKIFF, KEEPER OF GAY HEAD LIGHTHOUSE

The keeper of Gayhead lighthouse in 1805 made this petition for an increase of salary:

"Gayhead" October 25, 1805.

"Sɪʀ: Clay and Oker of different colours from which this place derived its name ascend in a Sheet of wind pened by the high Clifts and catch on the light House Glass, which often requires cleaning on the outside— tedious service in cold weather, and additional to what is necessary in any other part of the Massachusetts.

"The Spring of water in the edge of the Clift is not sufficient. I have carted almost the whole of the water used in my family during the last Summer and until this Month commenced, from nearly one mile distant.

"These Impediments were neither known nor under Consideration at the time of fixing my Salary.

"I humbly pray you to think of me and (if it shall be consistent with your wisdom) increase my Salary.

"And in duty bound I am your's to Command

"Eʙᴇɴᴇᴢᴇʀ Sᴋɪꜰꜰ,
Keeper of Gayhead Light House.

"Aʟʙᴇʀᴛ Gᴀʟʟᴀᴛɪɴ Eꜱǫᴜɪʀᴇ
"Secretary of the Treasury."

In consequence of this letter President Jefferson approved of increasing his salary by $50 to $250 per annum.

A SECTION OF THE BASE OF THE EDDYSTONE TOWER
The stones are dovetailed so as to withstand the terrible buffeting of the sea.

Ten years later the same Ebenezer Skiff petitions for an increase of salary on these grounds, some of which have a familiar ring, although the spelling has somewhat changed. The letter is quoted in full, as of interest in showing the life of a light-keeper at that date:

"To Samuel Smith Esquire
Commissioner of the Revenue
"SIR: Clay ochre and earth of various colours from which this place derived its name ascend in a sheet of wind from the high clifts and catch on the glass of the light-house, which glass requires to be often cleaned on the out-side:—Tedious service in cold weather and not so commonly necessary in any other place in the Massachusetts, nor in any of the New Eng-land States.

"The Spring of water in the edge of the clifts, by means of their late caving has become useless. I cart the water used in my family more than half a mile, necessarily keep a draught horse and carriage for that purpose and fre-quently have to travel in a hilly common extending five miles to find the horse. Truely I catch some rainwater and it is as true that many times I empty it coloured as red as blood with oker blown from the clifts.

"My firewood is brought from the Main-land and, there being neither harbor nor wharf here, is more expensive than in seaports. Keep-ers in some places get their wood with little cost; but here the native Indians watch the shores to take all drifts.

"The lately constructed light with a stone revolves by a clock which is to be stopped every

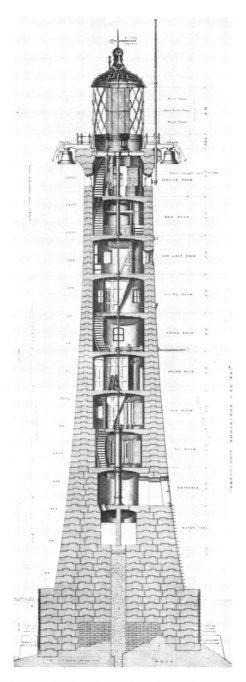

A SKETCH OF THE INTERIOR OF THE EDDYSTONE LIGHTHOUSE
Showing the foundation, dovetailing of stones, and interior arrangement.

PRESENT STONE LIGHTHOUSE ON MINOTS LEDGE, MASSACHUSETTS:
NOTE THE BREAKING SURF

This structure ranks among the difficult lighthouse engineering works of the world. During the first summer only 130 working hours were obtained on the rock, and after three years' work only four stones of the foundation had been laid. Commenced in 1855 and completed in 1860 (see page 21).

time anything is done to the fire, which, in cold weather, must be kindled the sun an hour high, or sooner, and recruited until eleven o'clock, or after, when I have to trim the lamps and wind up the weights of the clock and can go into bed at nearly midnight until which a fire is kept in the dwelling-house consuming more wood than when I tended the former light.

"It is about eight miles from here to a gristmill and in the common way of passing are creeks not fordable at all seasons.

"The business respecting the light is, mostly, done by me in person, yet I occasionally leave home to procure wood and many other necessaries; previous to which I have to agree with and instruct some trusty white person to tend the light in my absence: If my salary would admit I would hire some person to live constantly with me lest I should be sick—I have no neighbors here but Indians or people of colour.

"Tending the former light might be deemed a simple business if compar'd with the tendance of the present complicated works and machinery, which requires much time care &c.

"Almost any man or lad under my wife's care could light the former lamp and do the business a short time; but the case is not so now.

"When I hire an Indian to work I usually give him a dollar per day when the days are long and seventy five cents a day when the days are short and give him three meals: Now supposing the meals worth twenty-five cents each they amount to seventy five cents which is seven cents more than the wages for my service both a day and night (while I board myself) only sixty eight cents, computing my Salary (as it now is) at two hundred and fifty dollars a year and the year to consist of three hundred and sixty five days.

"I have the use of two acres of land intersected with buildings, the use of a small dwellinghouse and a small barn.

"I refer you to Capt. Winslow Lewis Superintendent of the Lamps &c. for the truth respecting all of the above particulars that he is acquainted with—and before I forward this Application shall lay before the Selectmen of Chilmark, which adjoins Gay Head, for their inspection; And in duty bound I humbly pray you to take this Matter into your wise consideration and afford me relief by granting an increase to my Salary.

"Gay Head 2nd November 1815.

"I am Sir with all possible respect yours to command.

"Ebenezer Skiff."

As a result of this letter, President Madison approved of a further increase of $50 in his salary.

CHARACTERISTIC ENDORSEMENTS BY JEFFERSON

On a recommendation to appoint Jared Hand as keeper of Montauk Point light to succeed his father, President Jefferson wrote this endorsement:

"I have constantly refused to give in to this method of making offices hereditary. Whenever this one becomes actually vacant, the claims of Jared Hand may be considered with those of other competitors.

"Thomas Jefferson."

In a matter respecting the conduct of the keeper of Cape Henry lighthouse he wrote:

"I think the keepers of light houses should be dismissed for small degrees of remissness, because of the calamities which even these produce; and that the opinion of Col. Newton in this case is of sufficient authority for the removal of the present keeper.

"Th. Jefferson.
"Dec. 31, '06."

LOCATION AND CONSTRUCTION OF LIGHTHOUSES

The first-class light and fog-signal stations are located at the more prominent and dangerous points along the seaboard, and on a well-lighted coast such stations should be sufficiently close that a coasting vessel may always be in sight of a light. The smaller lights are placed to mark harbors, inside channels, and dangers. Along the navigable rivers numerous post lights are maintained to indicate the channels.

STANNARD ROCK LIGHT, MICHIGAN

Built in 11 feet of water, 24 miles from the nearest land, it marks the most dangerous reef in Lake Superior. It is the most distant from shore of any lighthouse of this country.

For New York harbor and immediate approaches alone 268 aids to navigation are required, including 46 shore lights, 2 light vessels, and 36 lighted buoys; there are 192 buoys of all classes and 37 fog signals, including sounding buoys.

A chart of New York harbor in 1737 shows not a single aid to navigation there at that time. One may imagine the difficulties of Henry Hudson when in 1609 he sailed into New York Bay in the *Halfmoon*. The diary says: "We found it to have a very shoald barre before it;"

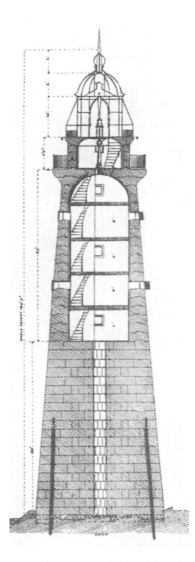

SECTION OF MINOTS LEDGE LIGHTHOUSE
Showing fastening of stones and interior arrangement. It is 107 feet from base to summit.

and, again, "the mouth of that land hath many shoalds." Boats were repeatedly sent ahead to sound as the *Halfmoon* worked her way into the harbor and river.

The natural alterations in channels and coast lines, the progress of improvements, and the changes in the trend and character of commerce and shipping make numerous modifica-

THE TILLAMOOK ROCK LIGHT COMPLETED

The seas here are terrific. On October 19, 1912, a wave broke a pane of the lantern 132 feet above the sea (see page 25).

tions necessary in the aids to navigation, so that this is a work that will never be complete while nature and man are active. During the past year notices have been published of about 1,600 distinct changes in aids to navigation maintained by the United States Lighthouse Service.

Among the lighthouses of the country may be found examples of great engineering skill and of dignified and simple design. Some of the tall lighthouse structures are of beautiful architecture, suited to the purpose, and set off by picturesque location on headland or rock overlooking the sea. The tower must be built to give the light a suitable height above the water, and hence tall lighthouses are required on low-lying coasts.

A light must be about 200 feet above the water to be seen from the deck of a vessel 20 nautical miles distant; beyond that distance the curvature of the earth would prevent a light at this elevation being seen. The light and lens are protected by an outer lantern of glass.

At the principal stations provision is made either in the tower or in separate buildings for the mechanical equipment connected with light and fog signal, for storage of oil and supplies, for quarters for keepers and their families, boats, etc.

Various materials have been employed in lighthouse construction—stone, brick, iron, steel, concrete, reinforced concrete, and wood; in new work, however, the latter is now little used because of the desirability of permanency.

BUILDING THE LIGHTHOUSE ON ST. GEORGE REEF, CALIFORNIA

The rock is so exposed that the workmen were obliged to live in the schooner, moored beside the rock, and were carried back and forth by a traveler on a cable (see page 27).

The Lighthouse Service at present owns 1,186 distinct pieces of land; besides this, many lights stand in the water, and post lights along the rivers are on temporary sites not purchased.

WONDERFUL
SEA-SWEPT LIGHTHOUSES

Lighthouse construction on the land is usually comparatively simple, except when there is difficulty of access to the site. But often it is important for the protection of shipping that lighthouses be erected either on rocks or reefs exposed to the sea or actually in the water, on sand or rock bottom. Such work has called forth the greatest skill of engineers.

Numerous types of construction have been used. Where the foundation is exposed, even at the lowest tides, masonry towers have been, with great labor and often danger, fitted to the bed-rock; otherwise the structure has been erected on iron piles driven, screwed, or pumped into the sand or coral, or on caissons floated to the site and set on the bottom or sunk deeper by the pneumatic process, or by the use of coffer-dams, within which the masonry tower has been erected; smaller structures have been placed on rip-rap foundations.

The earliest example now existing of a sea-swept lighthouse is the beautiful tower of Cordouan, built in 1584 to 1611, on a rock in the sea at the mouth of the Gironde, on the west coast of France. This lighthouse has since been altered and raised in height. The original structure was elaborately decorated, and one floor was occupied by a chapel (see page 8).

The most famous of the sea-swept lighthouses is the Eddystone, 13 miles from Plymouth harbor, England. This was completed in 1699, after four years of work. During the first year all that was accomplished was drilling 12 holes in the rock and fastening irons in them.

ST. GEORGE REEF LIGHT, CALIFORNIA, COMPLETED:
A DIFFICULT AND EXPENSIVE STRUCTURE

This lighthouse, with the keepers and the engineer who built it, disappeared in the great storm of November, 1703, and since that time three other lighthouses have in succession been erected on the Eddystone (see pages 12-13).

MINOT'S LEDGE LIGHT

The earliest lighthouse built in this country in a dangerous position, exposed to the open ocean, was that on Minots Ledge, a reef off Boston harbor which had long been a terror to mariners. This was an open-work iron-frame structure, supported on wrought-iron piles wedged into holes 5 feet deep, drilled in the rock, which was bare only at low water. It was completed in 1848 (see page 15).

There was a great gale in April, 1851. "The light on the Minot was last seen from Cohasset on Wednesday night at 10 o'clock. At 1 o'clock Thursday morning, the 17th, the light-house bell was heard on shore, one and one-half miles distant; and this being the hour of high water, or rather the turn of the tide, when from the opposition of the wind and the tide it is supposed that the sea was at its very highest mark; and it was at that hour, it is generally believed, that the light-house was destroyed; at daylight nothing of it was visible from shore, and hence it is most probable it was overthrown at or about the hour named." Two keepers were in the tower and were lost, and this extract from the official report tells the story of one of the great lighthouse tragedies.

The present massive stone lighthouse was built on the same site on Minots Ledge, commenced in 1855 and completed in 1860. It

A TUG TOWING A CAISSON TO BE SUNK FOR A LIGHTHOUSE FOUNDATION
(SEE PAGES 23 AND 30)

ranks among the difficult lighthouse engineering works of the world. During the first summer only 130 working hours were obtained on the rock, and after three years' work only four stones of the foundation were laid. The reef rock was prepared to fit the stones of the lower courses and the latter were cut to interlock. Dwellings for the keepers' families were built on the shore, accommodations for the men only being provided in the tower.

Longfellow visited Minots light in 1871, and in a letter thus describes it: "The lighthouse rises out of the sea like a beautiful stone cannon, mouth upward, belching forth only friendly fires."

SPECTACLE REEF
AND STANNARD ROCK

Spectacle Reef lighthouse, built on a reef near the northern end of Lake Huron, is a stone tower standing in a depth of 11 feet of water, 10 statute miles from land. It is in a position exposed to heavy ice action. A coffer-dam was constructed at the site, the water was pumped out, the bed-rock was leveled off, and the lighthouse was constructed of cut stone, securely fastened. It was completed in 1874, and is a notable engineering work. The first year it was well tested by the ice. When the keepers returned to the tower in the spring of 1875 they found the ice piled against it to a height of 30 feet. As this was 7 feet above the doorway, they had to cut through the ice to enter.

Stannard Rock light, 24 statute miles from the nearest land and marking the most dangerous reef in Lake Superior, is the most distant from shore of any lighthouse in this country. It was completed in 1882, constructed in a manner similar to that on Spectacle Reef, and stands in the same depth of water—11 feet (see page 17).

THE 14-FOOT BANK LIGHTHOUSE, DELAWARE

The first lighthouse in this country, the foundation of which was placed by pneumatic process. Completed in 1887. The diagram shows men working in the caisson under air pressure removing the sand, which is blown out (see page 30).

CAPE HENRY FOG SIGNAL, VIRGINIA

This fog signal is an air siren driven by oil engines. The trumpets are curved downward to prevent sand drifting into the sirens. "The fog signals now in use in the United States consist of sirens, whistles, reed trumpets, aerial bells, and submarine bells. Sirens and whistles are operated by compressed air or steam, and trumpets by compressed air. To furnish air, compressors driven by internal combustion engines are used, and for steam signal boilers are employed. The larger fog bells, up to 4,000 pounds, have hammers actuated by a weight and clockwork" (see page 53).

WHITE SHOAL LIGHT

White Shoal, a dangerous spot in Lake Michigan at the entrance to the Straits of Mackinac, was marked for 19 years by a light vessel anchored over it. On account of the ice, this vessel could not be kept on the station during a portion of the season of navigation in the spring and fall. As the unmarked shoal was a serious menace to navigation at these seasons, an appropriation was made for building a lighthouse, and this was completed in 1911 at a cost of $225,000.

A timber crib 72 feet square and 18 feet high was built on shore and floated out to the site, where the depth of water was 22 feet. The bottom, which is of coarse gravel, was covered with 2 feet of rock, and the crib was filled with stone and sunk. Above this was built a concrete pier, which supports the lighthouse.

The light is of 1,200,000 candle power, flashing white every 8 seconds. In addition to the compressed air fog-whistle there is a submarine bell signal, located in 60 feet of water three-quarters of a mile from the station. This bell is supported on a tripod standing on the

THE PRESENT LIGHTHOUSE AND THE OLD ABANDONED
LIGHTHOUSE AT CAPE HENRY, VIRGINIA (SEE PAGE 31)

bottom of the lake, is operated by electric power transmitted through a cable from the light station, and strikes "23."

TILLAMOOK ROCK—ONE OF THE MOST EXPOSED IN THE WORLD

Two lighthouses involving great difficulties have been built on rocky islets off the Pacific coast—Tillamook Rock, completed in 1881, and St. George Reef in 1891. Tillamook is a high, precipitous rock south of the Columbia River and about a mile from shore. It is exposed to the sweep of the Pacific Ocean. Landing on the rock was very dangerous, and the foreman

was drowned the first day a working party was landed. There was serious difficulty in providing any protection on the rock for the workmen. It was necessary to blast off the top of the rock to secure sufficient room for the lighthouse (see page 19).

This light station is one of the most exposed in the world. The tower is 136 feet above high water, but the keepers reported that in a storm in 1887 the seas broke over the building, some going above the tower, and serious damage was done. In another storm *a mass of concrete "filling weighing half a ton was thrown over the fence into the enclosure," at a level of 88 feet above the sea.*

SOMBRERO KEY LIGHT, FLORIDA

A pyramidal iron skeleton tower, supported on iron piles driven into the coral reef. The keepers live in the house (see page 29).

Here is the keeper's report of a storm in October, 1912, at Tillamook light. The lighthouse tender, on account of weather conditions, was not able to reach the rock for 7 weeks after this storm:

"I regret to state that on the evening of the 18th, or morning of the 19th, we lost a portion of the west end of the Rock, water and rocks coming over with so much noise we could not tell when, and did not know it had departed before next morning when the sea went down so that we could go outside.

"At 12:35 a.m. on the 19th the sea came up and broke one pane in of the middle section of the lantern (132 feet above the sea), which also put the light out and flooded the watch-room, as well as down-stairs. To add to it all the soot and ashes came out of the stove in the kitchen.

"At 12:50 a. m. we had the light burning and storm pane in for the rest of the night.

"Siren was running until the crash came, but making no regular blast on account of the water filling the trumpet too fast. After getting the light burning we closed down the fog sig-

THE OLD AND THE NEW LIGHT TOWERS AT CAPE CHARLES, VIRGINIA

The tower on the right was built in 1864, but was abandoned in 1895, as the site was destroyed by erosion of the sea. The previous tower, built in 1827, had been discontinued in 1863 for the same reason. The new tower, shown on the left, consists of an iron cylinder surrounded by iron framework (see page 33).

nal, as the wind hauled to westward and cleared the atmosphere somewhat. Shortly afterward when taking siren out to clear it I found it filled partly full with rocks; therefore the water could not get out of it (siren horns are 95 feet above the sea).

"Will also state that every one under my charge worked hard and faithfully, regardless of water and glass, everybody being drenched to the skin."

Before the location of the lighthouse, this rock had been a favorite resort of sea lions, who completely covered its slopes; these at first were hostile and disposed to object to other use of the rock, but finally retired to other resorts.

ST. GEORGE REEF LIGHT, CALIFORNIA

St. George Reef light is built on a rock lying 6 miles off the northern coast of California. The rock was so exposed and swept by the seas that workmen could not safely live upon it, and it was necessary to moor a schooner near the rock to provide quarters for the men, who

THE PETIT MANAN LIGHTHOUSE, MAINE

A granite tower, 115 feet high. The light is white, fixed and flashing, showing a steady light for 1 minute, and a 5-second flash in the next minute. The fog signal is a steam whistle giving each minute two blasts of 5 seconds each.

were transported back and forth by a traveler on a cable. The total cost of the work at St. George Reef was about $712,000, making it the most expensive lighthouse that has been built in this country. These two exposed light stations on the Pacific coast are the only ones having five keepers (see page 20).

Of lighthouses built on piles in the water, the original Minots Ledge structure has been mentioned. Brandywine Shoal light, in 6 feet of water in Delaware Bay, completed in 1850, was the first in the United States built on iron screw-piles. These were bored down 6 feet into the sand bottom, the broad screws at the ends of the piles also furnishing additional bearing surface; this structure has stood 62 years, but now must be rebuilt on account of the piles having been damaged by the ice.

THE ST. JOHNS RIVER LIGHT, FLORIDA

A brick lighthouse at the entrance to St. Johns River. A fixed white light, without fog signal. This light was recently changed from an oil wick lamp to an incandescent oil vapor lamp, increasing the candle power from 860 to 13,000.

LIGHTS ON THE FLORIDA REEFS

Five pyramidal iron skeleton lighthouses have been built in the water along the Florida reefs; these are supported on iron piles forced about 10 feet into the coral rock or sand. The piles are driven through large cast-iron discs, with a shoulder bearing on the disc; these discs are about 8 feet in diameter and give a broad support for the structure.

Sombrero Key, with its light 142 feet above the sea, is the tallest of these reef light-

houses (see pages 25 and 26). The keepers' quarters are carried within the skeleton tower, and they thus live 37 feet above the water.

LIGHTS ON SAND BOTTOM— THE 14-FOOT BANK LIGHT

The first lighthouse built in the sea distant from the land and not on a rock foundation was the Rothersand. This notable engineering work stands in 20 feet of water, on a sand foundation, in the North Sea, 10 miles from the German

THE PIGEON POINT LIGHTHOUSE, ON THE RUGGED PACIFIC COAST, CALIFORNIA

This light gives each 10 seconds a flash of 4 seconds' duration and 160,000 candle power. The fog signal is a first-class air siren, giving each 30 seconds two blasts in quick succession.

coast, in the approach to Bremen. The first attempt to place a lighthouse in this position resulted in failure, but a structure was finally completed in 1885.

A caisson of boiler iron 36 feet wide 46 feet long, and 61 feet deep was built in port. This caisson was towed to the site and sunk in position. Eight feet above the lower or cutting edge of the caisson was a diaphragm, forming a working chamber, from the center of which rose a cylindrical shaft with an airlock. The caisson was sunk by the pneumatic process to a depth of 73 feet below low water, the sand

being removed from the working chamber by a sand blast; the caisson was filled with concrete and masonry and the light-tower erected on this foundation.

Two years later, in 1887, the first lighthouse in the United States built on a submarine foundation and sunk in a sand bottom by the pneumatic process was completed on Fourteen-foot Bank, Delaware Bay, in 20 feet of water. A timber working chamber 40 feet square was built, with cutting edge 7 feet deep. On this was placed an iron cylinder 35 feet in diameter and 18 feet high, built of cast-iron plates bolted

A POST LIGHT ON THE MISSISSIPPI RIVER
Post lights are maintained on about 5,500 miles of rivers in the United States.

together by their flanges. This was towed to the site and placed in position. It was sunk, by digging and blowing out the sand, to a depth of 33 feet below the surface of the shoal, the cylinder being built up until it was 73 feet high and filled in with concrete (see page 23).

Cast-iron cylinders have been used also on other shallow submarine sites affording stable foundations or on rocks nearly awash. Wooden cribs floated to the site have been similarly employed, an example of which is Detroit River lighthouse. Recently reinforced concrete caissons have been used, sunk in place on the bottom, for minor light stations.

FAMOUS SHORE LIGHTS

Cape Henry lighthouse, at the entrance to Chesapeake Bay, is an example of an iron tower built with cast-iron plates bolted together along their flanges. The old tower at Cape Henry, abandoned in 1881, was the first lighthouse built by the United States government, being completed in 1791. There is a letter dated December 18, 1789, from Governor Randolph of Virginia to President Washington, saying: "The State some years ago placed upon the shore at Cape Henry nearly a sufficient quantity of materials to complete such a lighthouse as

THE TALLEST LIGHT TOWER OF THIS COUNTRY, 200 FEET HIGH:
THE CAPE HATTERAS LIGHTHOUSE, NORTH CAROLINA

The spiral painting is to furnish a distinctive day-mark to mariners. "A light must be about 200 feet above the water to be seen from the deck of a vessel 20 nautical miles distant; beyond that distance the curvature of the earth would prevent a light at this elevation being seen."

was at that time thought convenient, which have been in the course of time covered by sand. Measures are taking to extricate them from this situation" and offering to sell the materials and cede the necessary land to the United States.

Petit Manan lighthouse, Maine, is a granite tower 115 feet in height. On Thatcher Island, at Cape Ann, Massachusetts, are two handsome granite light-towers, each 124 feet in height. St. Johns River light, Florida, is of brick 80 feet high (see page 29).

The tallest light-tower in the United States is that at Cape Hatteras, on the low-lying coast of North Carolina, which is 200 feet from base to top of lantern. The highest light, however, is that at Cape Mendocino, on the coast of California, which is shown 422 feet above high water; it is on a cliff, the lighthouse itself being only 20 feet in height (see this page and 34).

The main channel range for the harbor of Charleston, South Carolina, is composed of two stations of historic interest, the front-range light being on Fort Sumter and the rear light in

THE TWIN LIGHTS OF CAPE ANN, MASSACHUSETTS

Two granite towers, originally built in 1789. The two fixed lights were established to furnish a distinctive aid, a purpose which now would be attained by a single flashing light (see pages 32 and 42).

the beautiful spire of St. Philips Church (see page 35).

LIGHTHOUSE DISASTERS AND PERILS

Many are the vicissitudes and tragedies that are connected with lighthouse history. Mention has been made of the destruction by storm of the first Eddystone and the first Minots Ledge lights, with the loss of all the keepers, and of the fact that the first Boston light was burned and finally blown up, incident to the operations of war (see pages 3 and 7).

The danger of fire is great. There is a quaint report by Jesse Tay, inspector of customs, of the burning on November 7, 1792, of Tybee lighthouse, the first built in Georgia: "About 2 o'clock in the morning the negro that trimed the lites went up to trim them and he discovered the lanthorn in flames he cry'd out the litehouse was on fier i jump'd up and run up Stairs . . . the glass and sinders was fawling so thick and it was so very hot i was not able to tarry half a moment and i saw it was in vain to attempt to save it."

Lighthouses are sometimes undermined by the encroachment of the sea. From this cause three successive towers have been built at Cape Charles, Virginia. The first was constructed in 1827, 700 feet from the then shoreline; this was abandoned in 1863, and the whole site has now been washed into the sea.

The second was built in 1864, also about 700 feet from the shore, but the sea continued to encroach until this now stands on the edge of the water.

The present lighthouse was built in 1895, about 3,600 feet from the shore, and is an iron cylinder 9 feet in diameter, surrounded and braced by an iron framework. This light flashes "45" every minute, four flashes in succession, followed by an eclipse, and then five flashes (see page 27).

Hunting Island lighthouse is a tower of cast-iron plates, built in 1859, about a quarter of a mile from the sea, on the coast of South Carolina. On account of the sea cutting away the end of the island, its position became unsafe, and in 1889 the lighthouse was taken down and reerected on a new site 1¼ miles distant.

THE CAPE MENDOCINO LIGHT, CALIFORNIA

This lighthouse is only 20 feet in height, but it stands on the edge of a cliff, and the light is 422 feet above the sea, the most elevated in this country.

Sand Island lighthouse, with keepers' dwelling, was built on a sand island at the entrance to Mobile Bay, Alabama. The hurricane of September, 1906, carried disaster along the Gulf coast, and this telegram was received from the lighthouse inspector: "Sand Island light out, island washed away, dwelling gone, keepers not to be found." The tower remained, and one keeper had, fortunately, gone ashore, but the other keeper and his wife perished (see page 37).

Point Arena lighthouse, California, was wrecked by the great earthquake of April, 1906;

it has been replaced by the first light-tower of reinforced concrete built in this country.

The foundation of Chandeleur light, on the coast of Louisiana, was undermined and the tower thrown out of plumb by a storm in October, 1893.

Thimble Shoal lighthouse, in Chesapeake Bay, was run into by a schooner recently, the structure broken, and the house and light destroyed by the fire which resulted. This is the second time the structure has been destroyed by fire, and it has been rammed a number of times by vessels and tows (see page 38).

THE RANGE LIGHTS FOR CHARLESTON HARBOR, SOUTH CAROLINA

These two lights in line form a range for entering Charleston Harbor. Both are of historic interest—the front light on Fort Sumter and the rear light in the beautiful spire of St. Philips Church.

TROUBLES FROM ICE, BIRDS, AND SAND

Winter seriously increases the work of maintaining aids to navigation; the spray or sleet freezing may completely envelop the tower in ice, obscuring the light until the lantern is cleared. In northern waters, where there is floating ice, many of the gas buoys must be removed in winter and replaced by spare buoys, over which the ice may pass without serious damage to the buoy. The spray freezes to bell buoys sometimes until the weight of the ice overturns them.

Most of the lighthouses on the Great Lakes are closed during the winter months, when general navigation ceases on those waters. There is risk to men and vessels in taking off the keepers in the winter gales at the close of navigation. In 1893 three lighthouses in Chesapeake Bay—Wolf Trap, Smiths Point, and Solomons Lamp—were swept away by the ice.

Sand creates difficulties at some light stations located among dunes or shifting wastes of sand. At Cape Henlopen the sand driven by the wind has cut deeply into the wood framing of the keepers' dwellings, and has ground the

THE CHANDELEUR LIGHT-TOWER, LOUISIANA, WHICH WAS
ABANDONED AFTER BEING UNDERMINED BY A TORNADO IN 1893

window glass so that it is no longer transparent; but the lantern of the light is too high to be so affected.

Even the flying birds make trouble at lighthouses, as the brilliant light so attracts them that they will fly directly for it, and striking the heavy glass of the lantern are killed and fall to the ground. At Cape Charles light the keeper has seen ducks fly directly through the lantern and fall to the floor cut and torn by the broken glass. Some lighthouses are fitted with bird-protecting screens around the lantern, as for instance at Mayo Beach light on Cape Cod. When Sabine Bank light, in the Gulf of Mexico, was increased in brilliancy by installing an oil vapor lamp, a bird-guard was found necessary because of the birds flying for the lantern, attracted by the more brilliant light.

FROM WOOD FIRES AND CANDLES TO OIL VAPOR AND ELECTRIC LAMPS

The early lighthouses were lighted by wood or coal fires burned in open braziers, and later by candles inclosed in lanterns; the resulting light was necessarily weak and fitful, and a large part was lost by being diffused in directions of no use to mariners. A coal fire was burned at the Isle of May light on the coast of Scotland up to 1816, and the famous Eddystone was lighted with 24 wax candles to 1811. Oil lamps were early used in this country, if not from the first lighting of Boston light. Fish oil, sperm oil, colza oil, lard oil, and mineral oil were in turn burned, increasing expense in each case compelling a change. Circular wick lamps, with a central current of air, were invented by Argand in 1782.

At the present time lamps with from one to five concentric wicks, and burning a high grade of kerosene oil, are used in a majority of lighthouses. About 610,000 gallons of oil are burned each year at the light stations of the United States, about 340,000 gallons of which are for lighthouse illumination.

For the more important lights the incandescent oil vapor lamp is now used, having been introduced by the French in 1898. In this

THE SAND ISLAND LIGHT STATION, ALABAMA,
BEFORE THE HURRICANE OF SEPTEMBER, 1906

THE SAND ISLAND LIGHT STATION AFTER THE HURRICANE

This storm washed away the island with the keeper's dwelling, and the keeper and his wife were lost (see page 33).

THE ORIGINAL THIMBLE SHOAL LIGHT STATION, VIRGINIA

THE THIMBLE LIGHT STATION AFTER A SCHOONER
HAD COLLIDED WITH IT AND SET IT ON FIRE

A temporary light is shown, pending the building of a more substantial structure, now under way.

THE RACINE REEF LIGHTHOUSE, IN LAKE MICHIGAN, COVERED WITH ICE

"Winter seriously increases the work of maintaining aids to navigation, the spray or sleet freezing may completely envelop the tower in ice, obscuring the light until the lantern is cleared. In northern waters, where there is floating ice, many of the gas buoys must be removed in winter and replaced by spar buoys, over which the ice may pass without serious damage to the buoy. The spray freezes to bell buoys sometimes until the weight of ice overturns them" (see page 35).

LIGHTHOUSE TENDER CROCUS JUST IN FROM WINTRY WORK
ON LAKE ERIE NEAR THE END OF THE SEASON OF NAVIGATION

Most of the lighthouses on the Great Lakes are closed during the winter months, when general navigation ceases on those waters. There is risk to men and vessels in taking off the keepers in the winter gales at the close of navigation" (see page 35).

lamp the oil is heated and then vaporized, and is burned mixed with air under a mantle which is made incandescent. This gives a much more brilliant light than the wick lamp, with a smaller consumption of oil.

For instance, this change of lamps recently made at Cape Hatteras light has increased the brilliancy of the light from 34,000 to 160,000 candle power while the consumption of oil has been reduced from 2,280 gallons to 1,300 gallons a year.

Electric lights are used at a few light stations only. The expense is too great to warrant the employment of electricity at many important stations. For some harbor lights it can be used to advantage by taking current from a local source of supply, and a light can thus be maintained in an exposed position and controlled from the shore.

The electric light at Navesink, on the highlands just south of New York harbor, is the most powerful coast light in the United States. This light shows each five seconds a flash of one-tenth second duration estimated at 60 million candle power. Although, on account of the curvature of the earth, the light itself cannot be seen more than 22 miles, its beam has been reported to have been observed in the sky at a distance of 70 nautical miles (see page 45).

LIGHTS THAT BURN FOR MONTHS WITHOUT A KEEPER

There has in recent years been a greatly increased use of gas as an illuminant for minor lights, such as unattended lighted beacons and lighted buoys; this is due to the facility with which gas may be stored or generated, the light

AN UNATTENDED FLASHING GAS LIGHT ON RICHARDSONS ROCK, CALIFORNIA
This light will flash every 3 seconds for seven months before it requires another charge of gas. This would be a difficult and expensive site on which to establish a regular lighthouse with keeper's quarters (see page 40).

burning for considerable intervals without attention. There are also a few coal or oil gas harbor lights, supplied from local sources.

There are in use a large number of acetylene gas-lighted beacons, supplied by tanks of gas of sufficient capacity to maintain a quick flashing light for five months without attention. In other acetylene lights the gas is generated from carbide at the station or in the buoy. Oil gas under compression is also extensively used for lighted buoys, having been first employed for this purpose in 1878. Some of the acetylene beacons are provided with a sun valve, which saves gas by automatically cutting off the gas supply during the time the sun shines.

A gas beacon has recently been established on Richardsons Rock, a wave-swept rock west of the Santa Barbara Islands, California. It would have been very expensive to build a lighthouse with keepers, quarters on this rock, so this flashing beacon was established to give present protection to vessels from the danger. This beacon, without attendance, will flash its warnings every 3 seconds for 7 months (or over

6 million flashes) before it requires another charge of gas.

Ten years ago the first light in Alaska was established; now there are 95 in that territory, and the rapid increase of recent years has been due largely to the facility with which flashing gas lights, unattended, may be established in that region, where it would be difficult and expensive to maintain keepers. At stations, however, where there are fog signals, keepers must be stationed, as there is not yet available a practical automatic fog signal for land use.

POWERFUL REFLECTORS, LENSES, AND PRISMS ARE USED

In order to increase the effectiveness of illumination, reflectors, lenses, and prisms are used to concentrate the light and throw it out either in a plane around the horizon or in a beam or limited arc, where it will be most useful. Parabolic reflectors were introduced about 1763, and to show around the horizon or to render the light more powerful it was, necessary to mount on a chandelier a number of lamps each with its own reflector. Thus in an early list of American lights, the number of lamps is given, as Boston lighthouse 14 lamps, and Sandy Hook 18 lamps.

The French physicist, Augustine Fresnel, beginning in 1822, revolutionized lighthouse practice by inventing a system of annular lenses, refractors, and reflecting prisms, all of glass and surrounding a single central lamp. Various forms of lenses designed on these principles, with further improvements, are now universally used in lighthouse work, varying from the simple lens lantern, with a single annular lens, to the great first-order lenses, built of many pieces of beautifully cut and polished glass.

Of such a lens the distinguished lighthouse engineer, Alan Stevenson, wrote: "Nothing can be more beautiful than an entire apparatus for a fixed light of the first order. It consists of a central belt of refractors, forming a hollow cylinder 6 feet in diameter and 30 inches high; below it are six triangular rings of glass, ranged in a cylindrical form, and above a crown of thirteen rings of glass, forming by their union a hollow cage, composed of polished glass, 10 feet high and 6 feet in diameter. I know of no work of art more beautifully creditable to the boldness, ardor, intelligence, and zeal of the artist."

With the most complete lenses about 60 per cent of the light is rendered useful, the balance being lost at the top and bottom and by absorption of the glass of the lens and the lantern.

The first lens in the United States was installed at Navesink light in 1841. The largest lens in this service is that at Makapuu Point light, Hawaii, which is 8¾ feet in diameter. The introduction of more powerful illuminants and quick-flashing lights, with lenses concentrating more of the light, has rendered large diameter lenses unnecessary (see page 47).

INGENIOUS METHODS TO DISTINGUISH LIGHTS FROM EACH OTHER

It is important that lights be so distinguished from each other as to avoid the possibility of the mariner mistaking one for another. To this end lights are distinguished by their number, color, intensity, or time of visibility. Before the introduction of flashing or occulting lights, in a few cases two or three light-towers were built close together to give a distinctive combination, an example being the two lighthouses on Thatcher Island, Cape Ann. This is an expensive method not now employed for new lighthouse work.

Color distinctions, especially red, have been widely used, but are not suitable except for minor lights because of the great loss of power; with the best color, red, the loss is about 60 per cent. For lights to be seen at close range, two lights are sometimes shown, one vertically above the other.

With the systems now available of flashing and occulting lights, it is possible to obtain a great variety of clearly distinguishable characteristics. The first revolving light was installed in Sweden in 1763. The earlier slow revolving lights are now generally superseded by lights giving a flash or various combinations of flashes at shorter intervals, or lights showing continuously except for short occultations. Quick-flashing lights were first introduced in France about 1892.

The most powerful flashing lights are arranged to have the entire lens revolve, the beam from each panel of the lens appearing as a flash as it sweeps past the observer. To obtain rapid and smooth revolution, the lens is mounted on a mercury float, and a lens weighing, with fittings, as much as 7 tons may make a complete revolution in 30 seconds.

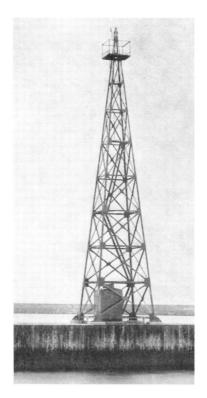

AN ACETYLENE GAS LIGHT, THE FAIRPORT WEST PIER LIGHT, OHIO

Gas tanks at base; light automatically occulting every two seconds. Sun valve to the left of lantern automatically cuts off the light while the sun shines.

A recent example is the lens for Kilauea light station, Hawaiian Islands, built in France and costing about $12,000, including import duty. The moving part weighs nearly 4 tons and turns on a mercury float, making a complete revolution every 20 seconds and giving a double flash of about 940,000 candle power every 10 seconds. The light is sufficiently powerful to be visible 40 miles but because of the earth's curvature it can be seen only 22 miles (see page 48).

Occulting lights are less efficient the occultations being obtained by revolving a screen around the light, by a drop shutter, or by blank panels in a revolving lens. With gas lights, flashes or occultations may be obtained by automatically interrupting the gas supply, a small pilot light still remaining.

The earlier lighthouses all showed fixed lights, and were equipped with lamps giving only moderate candle power. There is always danger of mistaking the identity of a fixed light, as it may be confused with other lights on shore or on vessels, or one lighthouse mistaken for another, and marine disasters have resulted from such mistakes.

VIEWS OF THE STATEN ISLAND LIGHT:
THE REAR RANGE LIGHT FOR AMBROSE CHANNEL, NEW YORK

The view of the interior of the lantern shows the fixed lens and reflector with incandescent oil vapor lamp. "For the more important lights the incandescent oil vapor lamp is now used, having been introduced by the French in 1898. In this lamp the oil is heated and then vaporized, and is burned mixed with air under a mantle which is made incandescent. This gives a much more brilliant light than the wick lamp, with a smaller consumption of oil. For instance, this change of lamps recently made at Cape Hatteras light has increased the brilliancy of the light from 34,000 to 160,000 candle power, while the consumption of oil has been reduced from 2,280 gallons to 1,300 gallons a year" (see pages 36 and 40).

All countries have, therefore, long since undertaken to change the fixed lights at important coast points and give them a distinctive characteristic, and also to increase the brilliancy of illumination.

To indicate the steady progress made along these lines, during the past two years this service has changed 47 lights from fixed to flashing or occulting, and at 68 light stations has substi-tuted incandescent oil-vapor lamps for oil-wick lamps, the latter greatly increasing the brilliancy, with a diminished consumption of oil.

DAYMARKS

In addition to the lights, many other marks are provided to assist navigators. The light-towers themselves are painted and shaped to

THE MOST POWERFUL LIGHT OF THIS COUNTRY,
ESTIMATED 60,000,000 CANDLE POWER: THE NAVESINK LIGHTHOUSE, NEW JERSEY

"The electric light at Navesink, on the highlands just south of New York harbor, is the most powerful coast light in the United States. This light shows each 5 seconds a flash of one-tenth second duration estimated at 60 million candle power. Although, on account of the curvature of the earth, the light itself cannot be seen more than 22 miles, its beam has been reported to have been observed in the sky at a distance of 70 nautical miles (see page 40).

make good landmarks in the daytime, and special beacons and spindles are placed usually to mark shoals or other dangers. Nature and man also provide many landmarks valuable to mariners' but which are not included in the official aids.

LIGHT VESSELS

All thus far mentioned are known as fixed aids to navigation, but it is frequently desirable to put marks in the water where the depth or other conditions do not permit of the building of a lighthouse or beacon. More than half the aids to navigation maintained by the Lighthouse Service are floating—light vessels or buoys moored in position.

Light-ships are placed in locations off the coast, where it would be impracticable or needlessly expensive to build a lighthouse, and they usually mark the approach to a port or bay or the outer limit of an offlying danger. They are also sometimes used in inside waters. They may be moored in the channel or close to it, and they have the advantage over most lighthouses, that a

AN UNATTENDED FLASHING LIGHT AT THE ENTRANCE TO PRINCE WILLIAM
SOUND: THE ZAIKOF POINT LIGHT STATION, ALASKA (SEE PAGE 40)

A LIGHT WHICH FLASHES EVERY 3 SECONDS
FOR 5 MONTHS WITHOUT ATTENDANTS

Many such lights have been installed to mark the inside passages in Alaska. This one is placed at Point Retreat, Alaska.

THE LARGEST LENS OF THE U.S. LIGHTHOUSE SERVICE

The lens is 8¼ feet in diameter, an occulting light eclipsed for 1½ seconds each 9 seconds. Makapuu Point Light, Hawaiian Islands.

vessel may steer directly for them without danger so long as collision with the light vessel is avoided, and also that they may be moved and moored in another position when change of conditions or necessity requires. On the other hand, a light vessel is more expensive to maintain, and there is the possibility of its being driven from its station, though this is reduced in recent years by improved vessels and moorings.

The first light-ship, the *Nore*, was established in England in 1732, at the mouth of the Thames. The first in this country was stationed in 1820 in Chesapeake Bay, off Willoughby Spit. Sandy Hook, now Ambrose, light vessel was established in 1823. A light vessel was placed off Cape Hatteras in 1824 and was driven ashore in 1827, and a ship was not established again in this dangerous position until 1897, after unsuccessful attempts had been made to build a lighthouse on Diamond Shoal.

The United States maintains light vessels on 51 stations, and there are a number of relief

A BEAUTIFUL GLASS LENS AND MOUNTING RECENTLY BUILT IN FRANCE FOR THE KILAUEA LIGHTHOUSE NOW UNDER CONSTRUCTION IN THE HAWAIIAN ISLANDS

It will be the landfall light approaching the islands from Japan. The light will give a double flash of 940,000 candle power every 10 seconds. The lens and mounting "weighs nearly 4 tons and turns on a mercury float, making a complete revolution every 20 seconds and giving a double flash of about 940,000 candle power every 10 seconds. The light is sufficiently powerful to be visible 40 miles, but because of the earth's curvature it can be seen only 22 miles" (see page 43).

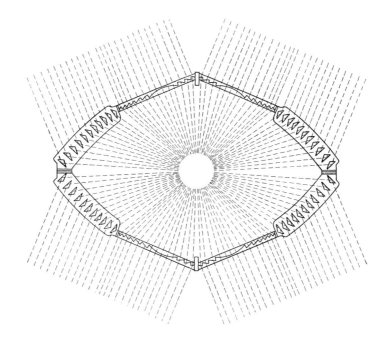

A CROSS-SECTION THROUGH THE LAMP OF THE LENS
SHOWN ON PRECEDING PAGE, SHOWING HOW THE LENS DIRECTS
ALL THE LIGHT OUT IN FOUR BEAMS, IN TWO GROUPS

ships, so that the regular ships may be brought in for repairs. Some of these positions are of the greatest importance to mariners, as, for example, the Nantucket Shoals light vessel, moored 41 miles from land, for which most of the transatlantic vessels steer in approaching America, and the Diamond Shoals light vessel, moored in 30 fathoms of water 13 miles off Cape Hatteras and marking the most dangerous locality on the Atlantic coast of the United States. These larger ships are full-powered vessels, capable of returning to their station, and they each have a crew of 15.

The latest ships are provided with powerful and distinctive lights and fog signals. They more nearly approach the lighthouse in design, having a heavy tubular iron mast surmounted by a lantern, sometimes with a revolving lens supported like a pendulum to hang vertically, so that the light beam will be kept near the horizon regardless of the motion of the vessel. An example is the recently completed Milwaukee light vessel, which will show a double flash every 10 seconds. This vessel has a fog signal giving two blasts each minute, with intervals of 7 and 46 seconds.

LIFE ON THE LIGHT-SHIPS

Life on a light-ship is somewhat dreary, but not without excitement. During every fog the crew on Nantucket ship know that numerous vessels are headed directly for them, and in a storm, anchored as they are in the open sea,

DIAMOND SHOAL LIGHT VESSEL, NORTH CAROLINA

This vessel is anchored in 30 fathoms of water in the Atlantic Ocean 13 miles off Cape Hatteras, and occupies one of the most exposed and dangerous positions. The vessel is shown after being stranded in 1899. The diagram below shows the improved method now in use of mooring light vessels with a submerged buoy.

they may be far from comfortable. The men in turn are allowed liberal leave ashore. There are often serious difficulties in getting coal and provisions to the ships on exposed stations, so that it is necessary that they carry sufficient supplies to last over stormy periods.

In 1899 the Columbia River light vessel was stranded near Cape Disappointment, and as it could not be gotten off into the sea again, it was hauled 700 yards across the land through the woods and launched in the Columbia River.

The light-ships, being necessarily near the channel ways, are frequently collided with. In January, 1912, a schooner ran into Diamond Shoal light vessel. The master, in his report, describes the damage done and states that "the 6 seamen and also the cook worked manfully all

night in trying to save the mainmast," and that "repairs having been made, the light having been kept burning as usual, and the ship kept in right position, unless very severe weather sets in the vessel will stay here until relieved."

The directions of the Superintendent of Lights in 1829 to the master of a light vessel instruct him "not to slip or cut the cable, or suffer it to be done, in any event, and if the vessel should be likely to founder, to abandon her with his crew."

Notwithstanding the severe conditions, Diamond Shoal light vessel has in recent years been maintained on the station with little interruption. The vessel is now moored with a 7,500-pound mushroom anchor and 150 fathoms (900 feet) of heavy chain. About one-third

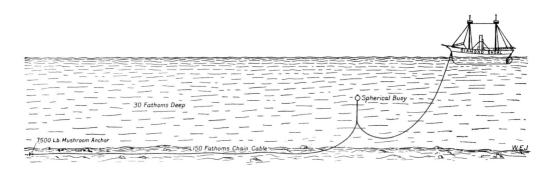

DIAGRAM SHOWING THE MOORING
ARRANGEMENT OF DIAMOND SHOAL LIGHT VESSEL

Length of chain on buoy, 7½ fathoms; from the anchor to buoy chain, 105 fathoms; from buoy chain to ship, 45 fathoms

of the length from the vessel a submerged spherical buoy is attached to the chain, carrying a part of its weight and greatly easing the pull of the vessel.

In recent years some unattended light vessels have been established abroad. These are small vessels without any crew and with all the apparatus automatic in operation. The Barrow light vessel, on the coast of England, with no crew, has an automatic flashing gas light with a revolving lens, a fog bell in the air, and a submarine bell, both actuated by the motion of the vessel in the sea (see page 55).

BUOYS

Floating buoys are efficient and relatively inexpensive aids to navigation. They are used to mark dangers—as shoals, rocks, or wrecks—to indicate the limits of navigable channels, or to show the approach to a channel. They vary in character according to their purpose or the distance at which they should be seen. The simpler forms are the wooden and iron spar buoys, and iron can and nun buoys. For warning in thick weather, buoys are fitted with bells,

whistles, and submarine bells, all actuated by the motion of the sea.

Some important buoys are lighted, usually by means of oil gas compressed in the buoy itself or acetylene gas compressed in tanks placed in the buoy or generated in it. The light is often flashing or occulting, for the purpose both of providing a distinctive mark and of prolonging the supply of gas. The use of gas buoys has greatly increased in recent years, there being at present 346 in this country. They are a very valuable addition to the aids for the benefit of mariners, and often obviate the necessity of establishing much more expensive light vessels or range lights on shore.

The buoy off the entrance to Ambrose Channel, New York harbor, at a height of 27 feet above the water, shows a light of 810 candle power, occulting every 10 seconds and visible 10 miles. This buoy recently burned for one year and four months without recharging. The buoy is nearly 60 feet long and weighs over 17 tons.

Buoys are painted and numbered to indicate their position and the side on which they should be passed. To keep the 6,700, buoys of

THE AMBROSE LIGHT VESSEL AND AN OCEAN LINER

This light vessel is anchored off the entrance to New York Bay. Ocean passages are reckoned to or from this ship. "Light-ships are placed in locations off the coast where it would be impracticable or needlessly expensive to build a lighthouse, and they usually mark the approach to a port or bay, or the outer limit of an offlying danger. They are also sometimes used in inside waters. They may be moored in the channel or close to it, and they have the advantage over most lighthouses, that a vessel may steer directly for them without danger so long as collision with the light vessel is avoided, and also that they may be moved and moored in another position when change of conditions or necessity requires. On the other hand, a light vessel is more expensive to maintain, and there is the possibility of its being driven from its station, though this is reduced in recent years by improved vessels and moorings" (see page 45).

THE NANTUCKET LIGHT VESSEL, MOORED IN THE ATLANTIC 41 MILES FROM LAND

Most of the transatlantic vessels steer for this vessel. "Life on a light-ship is somewhat dreary, but not without excitement. During every fog the crew on Nantucket ship know that numerous vessels are headed directly for them, and in a storm, anchored as they are in the open sea, they may be far from comfortable. The men in turn are allowed liberal leave ashore. There are often serious difficulties in getting coal and provisions to the ships on exposed stations, so that it is necessary that they carry sufficient supplies to last over stormy periods" (see page 49).

THE COLUMBIA RIVER LIGHT VESSEL, AFTER BEING STRANDED ON
CAPE DISAPPOINTMENT IN 1899, WAS HAULED THROUGH THE WOODS
700 YARDS AND LAUNCHED INTO THE RIVER (SEE PAGE 50)

this country on their proper stations and in good order is a heavy work and is one of the principal uses for the lighthouse tenders. Buoys may be damaged or sunk, or dragged or broken from their moorings by vessels or tows, or wreckage, or ice.

Two buoys from the Atlantic coast of this country have been picked up on the coast of Ireland, and one from the California coast was found in the Hawaiian Islands, these having gotten adrift and been carried: across the oceans by the currents.

For use in mooring buoys and light vessels, the Lighthouse Service purchases annually about 15,000 fathoms of chain, a length equal to 17 statute miles.

FOG SIGNALS

The most powerful coast lights may be rendered of little or no use to navigation by thick fog or rain. To assist vessels under such conditions, making their course more safe or allowing them to proceed, fog signals of many sorts have been established. Of these the bell is the most common, and until about 1850 the only signals in use were bells and guns. The first fog signal on the Pacific coast of the United States was established at Bonita Point, San Francisco Bay, in 1856—a fog gun to be fired each half hour.

The fog signals now in use in the United States consist of sirens, whistles, reed trumpets, aerial bells, and submarine bells. Sirens and

THE COLUMBIA LIGHT VESSEL JOURNEYING THROUGH THE WOODS

whistles are operated by compressed air or steam, and trumpets by compressed air. To furnish air, compressors driven by internal combustion engines are used, and for steam signals boilers are employed. The larger fog bells, up to 4,000 pounds, have hammers actuated by a weight and clockwork. The smaller bells are rung by hand. Besides the above, there are various noise-making buoys; bells, whistles, and submarine bells are attached to buoys and are made to sound by the movement of the buoy due to the sea.

THE MILWAUKEE LIGHT VESSEL, THE LATEST BUILT IN THIS COUNTRY

It has a hollow steel mast, through which access is had to the lantern surmounting it. The lantern will be fitted with a revolving lens giving a flashing light (see page 49).

AN UNATTENDED LIGHT VESSEL ON THE COAST OF ENGLAND

It has no crew, and is equipped with flashing gas light, aerial fog bell, and submarine fog bell, all automatic. The bells are operated by the motion of the vessel in the sea.

A BELL BUOY TAKEN ON BOARD LIGHTHOUSE TENDER

Shows marine growth and the necessity for periodic cleaning and painting of buoys.

There are also used abroad several other types of fog signals. The diaphone, similar to the siren, explosive signals, consisting of a tonite or other explosive fired from the top of a mast, and recently there has been installed, experimentally, at several light stations in France apparatus for sending signals by wireless telegraphy, and a compass has been invented which from a vessel will give the direction of the sending station.

Nearly all fog signals excepting those on buoys are operated to sound a characteristic signal so that they may be distinguished, there being a succession of blasts or groups of blasts or strokes at regular time intervals, which are made known for each station. Even adjacent buoys are differentiated by the use of whistles and bells and by variation of tone.

A first-class fog-signal station requires powerful and expensive machinery and skilled attendance. Such a station may have duplicate engines of 20 horsepower each, and the signal may consume 100 cubic feet of free air per minute.

While aerial fog signals furnish a very valuable aid to navigation under weather conditions when assistance is most needed, yet they are far from the ideal of perfection. Sounds are transmitted through the air erratically, and sometimes within a comparatively short distance of a station the fog signal may be inaudible, while in other directions it may be heard

GAS BUOY ALONGSIDE A TENDER, BEING RECHARGED WITH OIL, GAS
The great gas buoy off New York entrance with light 27 feet above the water, which recently burned for 16 months without attention, occulting every 10 seconds.

for long distances. This is due to the effect of the adjacent land or to conditions in the atmosphere, the sound being reflected or the sound waves deflected or retarded; the subject is one of importance, requiring further investigation.

There is sometimes an unfortunate conflict of interest between the need of a loud and distinctive sound to aid the mariner in a fog and the quiet and comfort of seashore residents in whose midst the fog-signal station may be located. Even the mournful note of the whistling buoy may bring complaints from the near-by shore residents.

Keepers at fog-signal stations must maintain a continuous watch day and night, as the signal must be started promptly on the approach of fog. Some portions of the coast have little or no fog, as on the south Atlantic and Gulf coasts, where there are but few fog signals; there are no fog signals in Puerto Rico or in the Hawaiian Islands. Fogs and thick weather are very prevalent on the New England and the Pacific coasts. At the station at Seguin Island, Maine, there were, in 1907, 2,734 hours of fog, more than 30 per cent of the entire year.

SUBMARINE BELLS

Submarine bells were first regularly employed as fog signals in the United States in 1906. The bell is suspended in the water from a light vessel to a depth of 25 to 30 feet and is operated by compressed air, or the bell is mounted on a tripod on the bottom and worked by electric power transmitted from the shore through a cable, or it is suspended from a buoy and actuated by the motion of the sea, which moves a vane and winds a spring (see page 59).

Sound from submarine bells is transmitted through the water more uniformly and effectively than it is through the air from an aerial signal, but the efficient use of submarine bells requires that vessels be equipped with suitable receiving apparatus attached to the hull on each bow and telephonically connected with the wheel-house; by comparing the loudness on the two sides the direction of the signal may be obtained. Submarine bells have frequently been heard through the water at distances of 15 miles and more.

LIGHTHOUSES MAINTAINED BY ALL COUNTRIES

As of the surface of the earth 51,886,00 square miles is land, as compared with 145,054,000 square miles of water, it is evident that a large part of the commerce of the world will always be carried on this great water area. Lights and buoys and fog signals are essential to safeguard the ships as they approach the continents and follow the coasts, and these or other suitable guides will be needed for aerial traffic, should it ever develop.

The proper lighting and marking of the coasts is an obligation assumed by all modern maritime nations. The lights protect not only the ships of the country maintaining them, but the vessels of other nations as well. The lighthouse, for instance, at Cape Maysi, on the east end of Cuba, is of great value to many ships which never call at a Cuban port. A lighthouse on Cape Spartel, Africa, at the entrance to the Mediterranean, is maintained jointly by the contributions of 11 nations, including the United States.

But there is a great difference today in the manner in which the shores of different seas are lighted. The official British lists give a total of about 11,600 lighthouses and light-ships for the entire world, but of these 8,900 are on the coasts of Europe, the United States, and Canada, while Asia, Africa, Australia, the remainder of America, and the islands of the sea have together about 2,700. South America has but 300 lights, and Africa 500.

A region of interest to our shipping, much of which is badly lighted and marked, is the area including the Caribbean Sea, the West Indies, and Central America. For example, the large island of Haiti has not a lighthouse at any one of its three prominent extremities. The only lights on Haiti are four harbor lights, which are marked in the list "not to be depended upon." A number of the lighthouses on the Central American coast are maintained by an enterprising steamship company.

Around the entire shore line of Bering Sea there is but one lighthouse—that at Cape Sarichef, Alaska—and some small lights near St. Michael; but this is a region where the commerce would not at present justify a costly lighting system, particularly as navigation is mostly confined to the season of no darkness at night.

It seems almost incredible to find, only three centuries ago, powerful opposition to the establishment of lighthouses. In 1619 a heroic Cornish gentleman, Sir John Killegrew, petitioned the king for permission to build a lighthouse on the Lizard, the southernmost point of

SUBMARINE BELL FOG SIGNALS

The submarine bell is suspended from a light vessel and operated by compressed air, or the bell is mounted on a tripod on the bottom and worked by electric power from the shore, or it is hung from a buoy and actuated by the motion of the sea. Sound is transmitted through the water more uniformly than through the air, and submarine bells have been heard at distances of 15 miles and more by vessels equipped with receiving apparatus.

England, where there is now an electric light whose powerful beam sweeps around the horizon. The nautical board to whom was referred the petition advised the king that it was not "necessarie nor convenient on the Lizard to erect a light, but, *per contra*, inconvenient, both in regard of pirates, or foreign enemys; for the light would serve them as a pilot to conduct and lead them to safe places of landinge; the danger and perill whereof we leave to your majesty's absolute and profound wisdom." Notwithstanding the flattery, James I granted the petition.

Next the local Cornish people opposed the work, as thus told by Killegrew: "The inabytants neer by think they suffer by this erection. They affirme I take away God's grace from them. Their English meaning is that now they shall receive no more benefitt by shipwreck, for this will prevent yt. They have been so long used to repe profitt by the callamyties of the ruin of shipping, that they clayme it heredytarye, and heavely complayne on me." The light was, however, completed and the fire kin-

dled, which, wrote Killegrew, "I presume speaks for yt selfe to the most part of Christendom." But it was impossible to obtain, for supporting it, the "voluntary contributions" from shipping which the king's grant authorized. Finally the corporation of the town of Plymouth pulled down the lighthouse, which the shipowners considered "burthensome to all ye countrie," and there was no light at the Lizard for 132 years thereafter.

Some of the early lights and buoys in England were maintained by religious men. On a tradition of such a philanthropy is founded Southey's ballad regarding the buoy on Bell Rock, where now stands a great lighthouse:

"The good old Abbot of Aberbrothock
Had placed that bell on the Inchcape Rock;
On a buoy, in the storm, it floated and swung,
And over the waves its warning rung.
"When the rock was hid by the surge's swell,
The mariners heard the warning bell;
And then they knew the perilous rock,
And blessed the Abbot of Aberbrothock."

A BATTLE-GROUND OF NATURE: THE ATLANTIC SEABOARD

BY JOHN OLIVER LA GORCE

Author of "Roumania and Its Rubicon," "The Warfare on Our Eastern Coast," etc.

THE operations of the sea assassins of Prussia on our eastern coast, in a futile effort to stay the mighty blow America is beginning to strike against despotism, brings into bold relief that ever-changing stretch of coastline we so proudly call our Atlantic seaboard, which the writer outlined in an article published in the September, 1915, issue of the GEOGRAPHIC.

As the crow flies, it is some sixteen hundred miles from the out-harbor waters of Eastport, Maine, to the keyguarded shallows of Cards Sound, Florida; but as the shore stretches southward, miles lengthen into leagues, rocky citadels give way to shifting sands, and both yield place to coral reefs.

He who would follow the foreshore from northern Campobello Island to southern Largo Key has a journey that while taxing his legs would certainly stir his soul, for in doing so he would traverse the length of a battle-front in the most ancient, the most far-flung, the most unremitting, uncompromising war ever staged between puissant forces of nature—the war between land and water, with the wind as a shifting ally.

This warfare, harsh in its local results, is yet one that by its analogies has comfort for suffering humanity in the present hours of stress and crisis, for the final results, however serious the momentary aspects, are beneficial to mankind.

Before visiting the various sectors of the seaboard battle-front to study the more intimate details of the war between the sea and the soil, let us endeavor to get a bird's-eye view of the great conflict that started long before man appeared upon the face of the earth, and which can only end long after the planet is no longer fit for his habitation.

Every coast-line on the globe, be it that of a great continent or a tiny island, is a theater of nature's struggle, in which the warring forces are marshaled; every rainstorm is a vast squadron of airplanes of the sea, a veritable Neptune's Escadrille, sweeping the shock troops across the No Man's Land of cliff, beach, and reef, onward to the very heart of the

A BELGIUM IN NATURE'S WARFARE: WOUNDED, BUT UNBOWED

land forces, strongholds, the mountains, where they wheel about and launch a rear attack with swollen torrent, hail, and ice.

Each drop of water is indeed a soldier of the sea, doing its small part, as it descends with force, in conquering the hillside, and its drum fire is to be reckoned with, because each inch of rain brings down one hundred and thirteen tons of water upon every acre of terrain upon which it falls.

THE AIR FLEETS OF THE SEA

As the tiny soldiers concentrate first in rivulet regiments, then into mountain-torrent divisions, and finally into big-river armies, they madly charge the rocks and grind them to dust by attrition and carry the captive sands ever onward to the sea.

The vast forces of the sea which are sent out in air fleets beggar belief. The rainfall of the United States perhaps averages 30 inches a year. On that basis every acre of ground is attacked by three thousand tons of water. And the water armies, marching back to the sea as rivers, take along a hostage of well-nigh unbelievable proportions, since it has been estimated that they carry some twenty-five billion tons of captive material with them.

The prisoners of the Mississippi might be used for an example, because their aggregate volume is greater every year than the total amount of material removed from the Panama Canal from the hour de Lesseps turned the first sod to the glorious day Goethals pronounced it a finished undertaking, or approximately 506,000,000 tons!

It often happens, however, that the seemingly vanquished turn on their captors just as they come down to the dead line of No Man's Land and succeed in saving themselves from the prison camps of the sea bottom.

In such cases they form themselves into river deltas, like those of the Mississippi, the Po, the Euphrates, and the Ganges, although our own seaboard captives are not so fortunate, since deltas are conspicuously absent from the river mouths of the North American Atlantic and Pacific coasts.

In the attacks of the sea upon the land via the air, it is the constant endeavor of the water forces to bring the whole dry land area under its liquid fist. If the sea ever succeeded in its program of world dominion, which includes dragging every mountain down and filling up every ocean trench with the material graded from the land in a leveling process, there would be a universal ocean nearly two miles deep over the face of the globe.

WATER'S ALLIES IN ITS AIR ATTACKS

The water has as allies ice and atmosphere in its air attacks upon the land. Seeking out the fissures in a cliff and filling them, the water waits until the frost comes and forms ice.

No giant of any age, no superman, imagined or real, ever put his shoulders against an object with such smashing invincibility as is evidenced in the forming crystals of a piece of ice, while the air, elusive, unsubstantial, as it may seem when compared with water, is yet no mean confederate, because with its power to attack through chemical transformation and its extreme mobility, it can work important results even in a brief campaign.

Yet more to the immediate point of this discussion is the frontal attack of the sea against the land. With wave and tide and wind and undertow, with coastwise current and ground swell, the sea pounds perpetually at the gates of the land fortifications.

Starting at Eastport, Maine, let us take a mental journey along the battle-front and

"THEY SHALL NOT PASS"
Artillery of the sea shelling a Verdun of the shore: Pulpit Rock, Nahant, Massachusetts.

watch the great drive of the sea and the defensive tactics of the land. On the northwestern shore of Campobello Island, that beautiful bit of British ground which forms the seaward wall of Eastport harbor, stands "Old Friar," a remarkable rock, isolated and solitary, alone with its memories of a bygone day.

It is but a different version of the "battle" rocks that dot the granite fortifications for many weary miles on this coast. These sturdy sentinels are isolated forces which have withstood the buffeting of the foe's advance and are the outposts of the land legionaries in their mortal combat with the wave army that sweeps the coast in relentless fury. Their supporting forces have fallen back, the watery foe has entirely surrounded them, yet boldly they defy his onrush and present an inspirational picture of adamantine resistance, as they break up the assault of the succeeding waves that rush against the main defenses.

Enduring, inflexible, they continue to hold where their weaker brethren yield territory inch by inch. No Ten Thousand Immortals, no Guard Regiments, no Macedonian phalanx, ever stood their ground more nobly than do the pulpit rocks of the Maine coast.

THE BATTLEMENTS OF THE MAINE COAST

We have not traveled far when we discover that the Maine coast is an unbroken series of steep battlements. Without power to advance, without mobility to shift their positions, these cliffs are destined to a defensive plan of campaign, while the waves possess initiative, and their generalship is of no mean order.

THE LAST STAND OF A LAND DIVISION
SOMEWHERE OFF THE COAST OF MASSACHUSETTS

Breaking relentlessly upon the eternal rocks, the waters: might still wage a vain war, did they not succeed in capturing from the cliffs stones and boulders which they use as projectiles when they return to the attack. Here hard, ungrained granite armor-plate stands in the path of the onrushing waves, with such undaunted and unconquerable strength that, smash as they will, hammer as they may, the waves retreat after their attack powerless to entirely reduce the defenses.

Farther along is another great mass of similar material, and it stands with corresponding might against the sea. But between them there is a series of cliffs made up of softer rock—the old men—and the young boys of the land forces. Their morale is not high, their strength is not great, and so they give ground.

The flanks hold, but the center yields, and alas, the untiring foe drives a salient into the lines of the land and uses the booty captured in his next drive. The salient is a bay or cove, and the wings are the headlands that bound it.

If one thrust be not too bitter, or if the retreating shore-line finally reaches a secondary line of defense on firmer ground, the enemy is held; otherwise it drives around the headland on all sides, and thus do "pulpit" or "chimney rocks" become lone outposts.

WHEN THE SEA ENCOUNTERS CROSS-FIRE RESISTANCE

It often happens, however, that when the thrust of the sea becomes too deep, the flanks of the attacking forces are exposed to the cross-fire

FATHER AND SON: CAPE HENRY, VIRGINIA

The old light tower was the first built by the American Government. The land army has defeated the sea at this point and driven it back nearly half a mile since the old light was established in 1791.

resistance of the headlands, and finally reach a degree of penetration where they cannot maintain communications, and their attack comes to a standstill. In such a case we have a deep bay where the rushing waves of the sea lose their force before they sweep the inner shore-line.

One does not have to study the warfare waged by the sea very long before discovering that it not only uses "pincer" tactics, but that it also makes use of mining operations. Sometimes it finds that its most powerful onrushes are dissipated by the resisting power of a great headland, as the dew is dissipated by the morning sun or the darkness by the light of day.

With boulder and shingle the waters drive furiously at the base of the cliff, tearing away its foundations inch by inch and foot by foot until a soft spot is uncovered, and the sea enemy finally undermines entirely the great structure of defense. Then with the hydraulic pressure of an imprisoned wave it heaves forward, and the rocks above have no alternative but to tumble helplessly into the maw of the liquid host, to become projectiles in the sea's further assaults.

Often, too, the rushing waves find a weak link in the armor where one ledge of rock overlies another, with gravel or clay between. Yard by yard they wear out this grouting material, and a sea cave is the result.

The ledges which constitute the roof and the floor, respectively, have a dip toward the sea, and as the waves rush in they come nearer and nearer to the surface, until finally they break through at some joint in the roof, and we have the spouting horn—a trumpeter of Neptune who gives the gage of further battle with each flooding tide.

At still other places the waves drive back the softer shore and bare a long stretch of adamant on each flank. And then it comes to a spot in this flinty headland that is weak, and

cuts its way through, making a graceful arch of a wonderful, wave-hewn natural bridge.

The tremendous power of the sea in utilizing the boulders it has wrested from the land in its return to the attack surpasses belief. Huge rocks, weighing seventy-five tons or more, have been moved by the power of the waves.

THE 42-CENTIMETER SHELLS OF THE SEA

Driving the big boulders up against the cliffs as though from a giant catapult, these 42-centimeter shells are finally worn down into cobble-stones, then into pebbles, then into sand, and at last into silt, which, caught up by the undertow, is borne along and out to sea, a bit of land forever in the prison-camp of the ocean.

As a result of the terrific grinding of the glacial ice of ages agone and in the following centuries under such methods of attack as have been broadly sketched, the Maine coast beyond Portland has become a series of gulfs and bays and headlands, with islands and rocks without number as the observation posts and firstline defense against the sea.

From Portland to Newburyport the bold cliffs gradually lower their towering forms and beaches and broad bays appear (see page 72). From Newburyport to Woods Hole is about eighty-five miles in a bee-line, but if you follow the shore around Cape Cod Bay and down along Nantucket Sound it is some three hundred miles. In that stretch of coastline one might see fairly good types of all the shores from Greenland to Florida. There may not be fiords like those of the far north or swamps like those of Virginia, Georgia, and Florida, but there are enough shore-line features to fascinate any pilgrim who would wander that way.

AN INNOCENT BYSTANDER CAUGHT BETWEEN THE BATTLE LINES

A GIBRALTAR OF THE AMERICAN SEACOAST

North of Gloucester lies Cape Ann, with her pocket beaches. Here the waves run high and dash themselves with unpitying force against the solid old rock; but she holds firm, a Gibraltar of the American seacoast, guarding the outer approaches to Boston, as the wonder-ful British fortress has stood watch and ward in the path of the invader of the Mediterranean. So wild is the sea here that it is said that a sharp-angled fragment of stone as large as a steamer trunk is often worn as round as a tennis ball in the course of five years.

Many a brick and coal laden ship has per-ished upon such shores as these, and their scat-tered pieces of cargo have been ground to bits

OBSERVERS ON THE BATTLE-FRONT OF
NATURE'S WORLD-OLD WAR: OFF THE VIRGINIA CAPES

under the incessant hammerings of one another under the surge of the waves.

Marblehead, on the northern shore of Massachusetts Bay, is worthy of its name, and often the sea resorts to unusual tactics in trying to conquer it. Shaler, the well-known authority on geology, tells of witnessing an attack in which the sea used seaweed as its ammunition train. Sometimes these plants grow in shallow waters and wrap their roots around boulders on the floor of the ocean. Then, as the surging sea rolls in, it lifts the seaweed on its buoyant bosom, and the plants in their turn tug at the rocks which their roots enmesh, until finally the boulders are lifted clear of the bottom and carried along into the maelstrom of attack.

It is too hard a struggle for the seaweed, which is quickly torn asunder, but the stones are driven up to the attack again and again. As much as ten tons of these seaweed-borne rocks are sometimes cast up upon a quarter-mile stretch of shore-line by a single storm.

A NEUTRAL OBSERVER SURVEYS FROM ALOFT THE
ETERNAL CONFLICT OF THE LAND AND THE SEA FORCES

COMMUNIQUES OF
NATURE'S WARFARE

Farther south, on the northern wing of the Atlantic battle-front, lies Lynn, and in the sea below Lynn lies Nahant Island, which bids us hope for here at last the sea has lost the initiative, the land has assumed the offensive, and in an inspiring counter-attack is demonstrating its ability to give blow for blow and to match maneuver against maneuver.

Indeed, here for the first time we are to learn, in Nature's War Communiques, that the hardest rocks of the northern coast are more yielding than the softest sands of the southern waters and, in spite of local engagements fought with fluctuating results in this or that sector, as a whole, the land is holding its own from Lynn to the silver sands of Alton Beach at Miami.

In the counter-attack in the Lynn sector the land has built up a sandy beach between Nahant Island and the mainland.

Passing the Boston sector, where comparative quiet has reigned for some time midway between Plymouth and Barnstable, where Buzzards Bay on the south and Barnstable Bay on the north have long seemed to conspire to tear off the "bare, bended arm" of Massachusetts, as Thoreau called Cape Cod, we come to the Cape Cod Canal. According to British charts in the Library of the United States Coast and Geodetic Survey, thought to date from 1715, there was once a sea-cut channel through that neck, and Cape Cod was an island, not a peninsula. Here, again, the land won out after years and tied an island to the mainland.

ICE AS A LAND ALLY

The Cape Cod Peninsula affords an illustration of how the ice in geologic times came to the aid of the land in its war against the sea. Once glaciers swept down from Labrador and Maine and deposited vast quantities of clay and boulders on the floor of the sea, making a great breakwater to the east of what is now Cape Cod Bay. This obstruction forced the sea to give up the stores of sand it was carrying, and with this material the breakwater gradually wrought itself into a peninsula.

Passing around Cape Cod's two shorelines, inner and outer, one comes next to Chatham, at the elbow of the outer shore. Here the sea is once more on the offensive, driving forward into the shoreline at the rate of a foot a year.

South of Chatham is Monomy Point, called by De Monts, the French explorer who nearly came to grief there in 1605, the "graveyard of ships," a reputation it has lived up to for three centuries and better. Looking southward across the eastern entrance to Nantucket Sound, one sights Nantucket Island in the distance. On the south side of this island the retreat of the cliffs is often as much as six feet a year.

Further to the west lies Martha's Vineyard, also an outpost of the land. Here there are rearing ramparts of rock a hundred feet high, but even they cannot entirely withstand the incessant attacks of the indomitable sea.

To the southwest of Martha's Vineyard lies the desolate island of "No Man's Land," which is well worthy the name it bears. Gradually the sea is tearing away its vitals, and it is predicted that by the end of the present century it will disappear beneath the waves forever.

In the case of the Cape Cod Peninsula, we saw how the land had used the ice of geologic times as its ally against the sea, but when we come to Long Island there is a different story. Here the ice negotiated a separate peace with the sea, and, sweeping eastward across New York, scooped out what is now Long Island

WHERE PRISONERS OF WAR ARE FORCED TO FIGHT THEIR BRETHREN

A typical sector near Highland Light, Massachusetts, where the sea enemy uses captured boulders, torn from cliffside defenses, as projectiles with which to batter down the ramparts. Note the prisoners "left upon the wire" at the beachline.

AN OBSERVATION POST ON THE FIRING LINE

The sea makes a desperate attempt to gain a foothold near Portland Head Light, Cape Elizabeth, Maine, but with little success.

Sound, thus enabling the enemy to isolate the island entirely from the mainland.

WHEN THE LAND ASSUMES THE OFFENSIVE

On the south coast of Long Island we find beaches and shifting sands. Here again we get into more hopeful territory, for the land always has an upbuilding Oliver for every down-tearing Roland the sea may have to offer. From Shinnecock Bay to Fire Island, a rampart of sand some 40 miles long has been thrown for-

ward off the real shore-line, and the sea, pounding against this in its maddest fury, encounters a buffer that throws it back a helpless and exhausted foe. Moreover, the sea is compelled to surrender captive sands taken up elsewhere, and these are re-equipped and put into the front trenches of the island's south-shore defenses.

Farther west on Long Island lies Rockaway Beach, the advanced line of defenses which the land has been throwing out to thwart the attack of the sea at the apex of the Jamaica Bay salient. What was once Pelican

A "TANK" ADVANCING OVER A FOREST

Sometimes, when the wind acts as an ally of the land forces, a heavy tribute is exacted from the sea, from which huge sand ramparts are built. Often these dunes, like great "tanks," become insubordinate and march inland, engulfing forests and even villages en route.

Beach has all but disappeared and what is left of it is now known as Barren Island. But Rockaway Beach has gained ground westward as fast as Pelican Beach has been driven eastward, and has now all but landlocked Jamaica Bay and its islands. It advances at the rate of two feet every three days.

SANDY HOOK AN ADVANCE GUARD

On the Jersey Coast, Sandy Hook stands out as an advance guard of the forces of the land, determined to cut through the line of communications of the sea in its drive into the Raritan Bay salient (see map, page 82).

"STAND TO ARMS"

There is little rest given the grim defenders of such a salient, for here the enemy force their prisoners, torn from cliff and beach, to advance with them in the wild assault.

When there is a deeply indented coastline, the ocean currents paralleling the shores refuse to follow the indentation and cut straight across. Striking deeper water, they slow up and deliver from bondage the captive grains of sand which momentum has enabled them to carry along.

Eventually these grains grow into a high submarine ridge, which holds up the onrushing waves and forces them to give up a sand toll as they pass. Having gained courage in its size, the ridge makes a sally from the surf and becomes a full-fledged spit, or hook.

Sandy Hook is a splendid example of this method of the land in invading the dominions of the sea. It very frequently happens that the spit marches on until it reaches across the bay area and captures the entire water army within the salient. Then science decorates it with a *croix de guerre* and gives it a new name—it becomes a bar.

The captured waters of Tisburg, Oyster, and Herring ponds, on the southern shore of Martha's Vineyard, afford an excellent example of the conquest of the sea by a spit. But the fortunes of war often change, and the Martha's

MOONLIGHT ON THE BATTLE-FIELD

Between the tides of attack a brief truce takes place between these world-old antagonists, but, as is the case in any undecided war with an unscrupulous enemy, it only means time in which to prepare for further attack at a later hour.

Vineyard Bar, once forcing a retreat of the open sea, is now in turn being driven steadily back. It is believed that the coastal edge at this point is a thousand feet from where it was when first seen by a white man.

WHEN THE SANDS ARE LED CAPTIVE

The Jersey coast is full of classic examples of the war between the land and the sea. Here are no towering ramparts with frowning walls, that seem to defy all the armies with which General Neptune can attack them. Nay, rather, here the land forces have camouflaged their strength, and have entrenched themselves behind barriers of sand.

At Long Branch one may watch the shifting fortunes of the battle. Here, in spite of the most elaborate system of breakwaters man has erected, the shoreline is being led captive inch by inch. But the prisoner sand does not remain in captivity. As it is being escorted back of the lines it makes a successful dash for liberty and rejoins other land units north and south of Long Branch and aids in a counter-attack in those neighborhoods.

It is hard to visualize the full meaning of the conflict's swing until one views the battle-field from the observation tower of history. A few feet won or a few feet lost in a year seem insignificant. But generations are merely short-lived seconds ticked off on the clock of geologic time, and one needs the sweeping view of centuries to appreciate it all. On the New Jersey coast we get a little of that.

Prior to the War of 1812, Old Cranberry Inlet was one of the best havens of refuge on the eastern coast. It was a safe harbor for American privateers lying in wait for enemy commerce. But one night the sea made a heavy concentration of forces and staged a night

attack of particular fury, broke down the defenses, and shifted the whole channel a mile to the northward.

SHIFTING OF LAND RESERVES AT ATLANTIC CITY

In the vicinity of Atlantic City the sea is ever striving to gain a foothold; but at present the best it can do is to force a shifting of land reserves from one side of a salient to another. In a few years it took off some 76 acres of ground from the neighborhood of Maine Avenue and forced most of it around to the lee of the point at Ohio and New Jersey avenues.

The pounding power of the waves when the sea is staging one of its major attacks is hard to picture by those who have visited the front-line trenches in bathing suits and have seen only a quiet sector. But when the breakers rush forward at a height of 10 feet or more, in serried ranks, striking from four to six majestic blows a minute, one does not wonder more at the vastness of the sea's reserves than he does at the land's powers of resistance.

SUBMARINES EMPLOYED BY THE SEA

The sea is thoroughly modern in its methods of warfare, even employing the submarine. As the waves sweep inward and break upon the shore, their waters must have some egress back to the deep. If they tried to go back as they came they would create confusion in the onsweeping forces behind them. To obviate this, they submerge and return along the bed of the beach. Here they constitute the undertow, an undersea current equally as reckless of life and the rights of noncombatants as a Hun U-boat itself.

It is by this route that they lead off many of their prisoners and drown them beneath the

A ROYAL BATTLE-GROUND: ORMOND-DAYTONA, FLORIDA

Here the White Horse Cavalry of Neptune make a charge twice daily over the most perfect beach in the world, from three to five hundred feet wide, on a front of about thirty miles. "The Silver Sands of Ormond" is no empty figure, because for ages the shells of the coquina clam have been ground under the heels of Neptune's charging horsemen until they have become fine sand. As soon as the foam-flecked forces fall back, the silvery sand settles down into a surface as level as a floor and almost as hard as asphalt, making one of the finest automobile speedways in the world, which is always kept in order by the tides.

waves of the sea. Ten thousand banks on the bottom of the deep are cemeteries peopled with the worn and wasted sands of the seashore which were carried there by the undertow.

If the sea in its warfare against the land sometimes ruins a haven of refuge, as it did when it broke through the lines of the land at Old Cranberry Inlet, previously cited, at other times it is compelled by the land to create such a haven.

Off the Maryland-Virginia shore lies the long, barrierlike island of Assateague. Once the seaward southern point of this island was only a bare lip. Gradually, however, the land began to force the sea to give it sand, and with this it has built a fine hook behind which many a mariner seeks safety from the fierce nor'easters that sweep these coasts.

From 1908 to 1911 this invasion of the sea by the land went forward at the rate of 200 feet a year. But latterly it is following the usual course of offensives and is now advancing at the rate of only 100 feet a year.

ANOTHER ALLY OF THE SEA IN THE VIRGINIA CAPES REGION

When one comes to the Virginia capes and studies conditions there, it is found that in times past the sea had another ally, of which no mention has yet been made—subsidences. In a bygone age the Susquehanna, the Potomac, and the James rivers rolled in stately grandeur to the sea. Then there came a subsidence, and the sea rushed in through the reach between Capes Charles and Henry and overwhelmed the land in all that vast area we call Chesapeake Bay.

The land has not always been without an ally to counterbalance this display of strength. Sometimes there come upheavals of the floor of the sea that drive the water into a retreat which often becomes a rout.

The consequences of even a slight upheaval may be strikingly shown by following what is known as the twenty-fathom line off the eastern seaboard. This line divides the sea into

ON THE WIRE: NO MAN'S LAND
WHAT SOMETIMES HAPPENS WHEN MAN DEFIES THE WARRING ELEMENTS

The sun is munition maker for the sea. Every day it sends to the earth enough heat to melt a cake of ice 5,000 feet thick and as large as the State of Massachusetts. This heat is the high explosive that puts the fury into the storm that drives the projectile waves to the attack.

two parts, that which is less than 120 feet in depth, and that which is deeper. Were the floor of the continental shelf, the vast, undersea platform upon which the continent rests, to rise 120 feet, Delaware Bay, Chesapeake Bay, Albemarle Sound, and all the other deep indentations of our coast would disappear and the new battle line would be practically without salients.

WHEN THE LAND SCORES A VICTORY

When the land is victor, through an upheaval, it always straightens out its battle front. The bed of the sea, being untouched by the chemical changes of the atmosphere, unharassed by running water, but constantly graded by deposits of sand in its low places and scoured by the tides in its high ones, is ever tending to assume a common level.

On the other hand, the land, attacked by chemical change, eroded by wind and running water, is an unending succession of elevations and depressions, and whenever there is a subsidence the sea seeks out every foot of ground below its level and occupies it.

Only the highest waves ever lash the sea bottom beyond a depth of 26 feet, and at 600 feet even the ripple-marks of a gentle surge disappear.

BARRAGE FIRE

Again and again the regiments of the deep advance to the attack with the wind ally behind them to whip the wave crests into stinging shrapnel.

THE WINDS A BOLSHEVIK ARMY

From the Virginia capes southward, one may see the same forces at death grips that are found on the Jersey and other coasts. But neither at Cape Cod nor in Jersey will one behold to such advantage the role played by the wind, the Bolshevik of the land and sea war, as in the region of the kingly capes and in the vicinity of Hatteras. Now it boldly marshals its forces alongside those of the water and urges on the attack with the utmost abandon. And now, repentant of that rôle, it steps in and helps the land erect great barriers of sand, against which the wildest sea, in its maddest moments charges in vain.

SUNRISE NEAR NORFOLK

The quiet waters of Norfolk's harbor have for nearly a century proved a welcome haven to ships from every out-of-the-way corner of the world; here the antagonists of the universe seem to have established a sort of unspoken peace.

The winds are the makers of dunes, the tanks in nature's warfare, and the humble beginnings of these mountains of glistening sand form a remarkable story. One who has stood on a sandy beach during a lashing hurricane and has felt the shining grains hurled into his face with a sting like that of a nettle, knows the wind's power and can the more easily believe the statement of scientists that a cubic mile of churned air may contain thousands of tons of sand.

Anything of substance, from a piece of wreckage to a tuft of grass, may be the nucleus of a dune that will grow and grow, broadening out as it rises higher, burying a forest, engulfing a house, or wiping out an orchard.

The trees which the sands seek to overwhelm put up a stubborn fight for life, but usually the dune is victor, and many are the places where one may walk through a graveyard in which a forest lies buried and only a limbless

A CAMOUFLAGED TRENCH

The enemy's thrusting-point is frequently changed and heavy artillery is superseded by strategy, during which period the land regiments endeavor to strengthen their fortifications by utilizing plant life to cement their trenches.

upper trunk has been left as a ghost of a brighter day.

Sometimes dunes migrate and the forest that was buried yesterday awakes to life tomorrow, for the wind picks up the sand it formerly laid down and drives it still further. Cemeteries have been first sheltered by a dune, then buried by it, then resurrected from it. On the Carolina coast a human graveyard has been despoiled by the shifting sands, and as the dune moved onward in its migration the very graves were opened by the force of the wind, and the bones of those who peopled them were left scattered on the soil.

WARFARE ALONG THE FLORIDA KEYS

The Carolina coast affords a striking example of the effectiveness of the wind as an ally of the land. Borne southward by the sweeping shore-following currents that come down from the north, sands that are the remains of boulders pounded loose from some rocky coast, have driven a wedge through the left flank of the ocean and have completely isolated the attacking armies holding the salients of the Albemarle and Pamlico sounds.

The winds have aided in the campaign and have piled up veritable mountains of sand

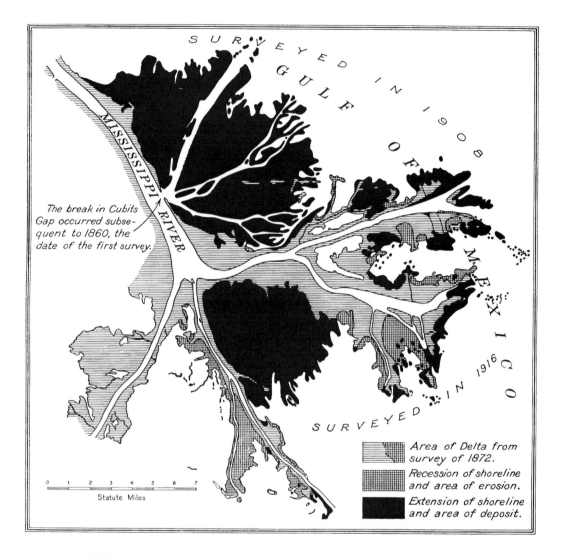

SKETCH MAP OF THE MISSISSIPPI DELTA SHOWING FORMATIONS

against future attacks by the sea. Thus the main battle line is straightened out and the enemy finds itself in a crossfire, with opposing forces athwart its line of communications.

Along the southeasternmost coast of Florida, from Cape Florida, which guards lovely Miami, on down to Key West, is the beautiful key region, where the coral polyps have established foundations upon which the land has been able to build first-line defenses that break up the assaults of the sea before they reach vital ground.

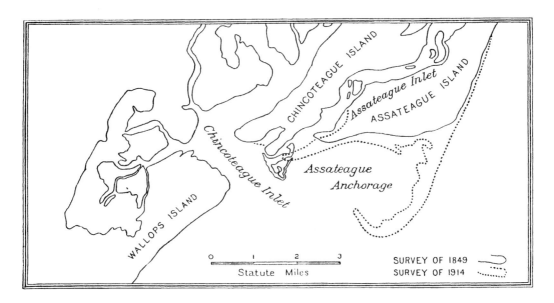

WHERE THE LAND HAS SCORED SIGNAL VICTORIES OVER THE SEA;
THE UPPER CHART SHOWS LYNN HARBOR (SEE PAGE 70);
LOWER CHART IS A SKETCH OF ASSATEAGUE ISLAND, VIRGINIA,
SHOWING LAND DEFENSES BUILDED SINCE 1849 (SEE PAGE 77).

Sometimes the water erects wonderful natural bridges in these barriers. On the western shore of the northern part of Biscayne Bay, which laves the shore of Alton Beach on one side and Miami on the other, a little river escapes from the Everglades to the elevated Barrier Reef through a beautiful rock arch cut by the water.

MAN AS A PROFITEER IN NATURE'S WAR

Thus having, with some little romantic license, outlined for the nontechnical reader the front-line trenches of nature's great war on our eastern coast, let us turn aside and see how man, the innocent bystander, the neutral, fares through it all.

In the attack of the sea via the air he is preëminently a profiteer. Without the water and atmosphere to weather the rocks of the mountains he would have no soil upon which to live, and without the rain that gladdens valley and plain the soil would be worthless.

But when it comes to the frontal attack he has to resort to many measures to maintain his neutrality and to prevent both belligerents from encroaching upon his domain. With his Lighthouse Service he warns the mariner of dangers ahead and directs the fleets of main and inland waters into safe channels. With his Coast and Geodetic Survey he plots the pitfalls and the safe shipways, so that the sailor may set his course without fear. With his Coast Guard he stands unending watch to help those who, in spite of all care, become entangled in the barbwire of

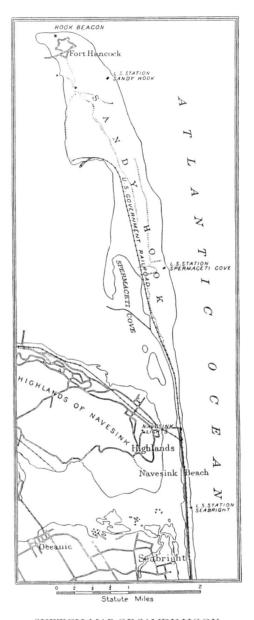

SKETCH MAP OF SANDY HOOK

A little south of Sandy-Hook, at Long Branch, the highlands yield a continuous supply of sand to the action of
the waves. This is washed up and down the beach with each advancing and retiring wave, but with each movement it is brought down to a place northerly of where it started, as the waves strike the shore obliquely and from
a southerly direction. So the sand is carried along until it is deposited in deeper water, where the wave action is
not so vigorous, gradually building up the bottom in much the same manner as a delta is built up at the mouth of
a river. Sandy Hook is the result of this action aided by the winds which blow the wave-brought sands into dunes.

THE SEA ATTEMPTING TO ESTABLISH A COMMUNICATION TRENCH ON THE
FRONT LINE OF BATTLE IN THE VICINITY OF CAPE HENRY, VIRGINIA

nature's battle-fields and would perish but for its timely aid.

BEACONS THAT GUARD
THE NEUTRAL'S RIGHTS

The most easterly light on the shores of the United States is that of West Quaddy Head. From there to the southern tip of the Florida coast there are scores of beacons of the sea, some with histories that warm the hearts of those thrilled by deeds of heroism.

The one at Mt. Desert is on a bold promontory where the pounding waves break high, and have been known to lash so fiercely that they moved a rock, estimated to weigh 75 tons, a distance of 60 feet during the fury of a single storm.

WHERE THE LAND ARMY HAS FORCED PEACE:
A PROTECTED HARBOR IN SOUTHERN WATERS

The Matinicus Light has a thrilling story to tell. Once the sea made a complete breach in the rock. Only the women-folk of the keeper's family were there when the storm broke, but little Abbie Burgess, fourteen, and her sisters stood up bravely against Neptune's outburst, and for four weeks kept the light aglow, although during that entire time there was not a moment when the government keeper, their father, could effect a landing from the near-by mainland.

The Minot Ledge light, standing far out on a lone rock, where the sea rounds Cohasset and speeds into Massachusetts Bay, has a striking history. For three years men worked like Trojans to build a lighthouse upon a barren rock. Its beacon flared forth for the first time January 1, 1850. A little more than a year later, in April, 1851, a great gale swept those seas. On the night of the 16th the light was last seen from Cohasset at 10 o'clock, and the bell was last heard an hour after midnight. When morning dawned it was gone.

But that tragedy only temporarily dimmed the light of Minot Ledge. A few years later the government completed the present massive stone structure, ranking among the greatest of the sea-rock lighthouses of the world because of the engineering difficulties surrounding its erection. A considerable part of the foundation was below low water, and landings could be made only at low spring tides in a smooth sea. Work was prosecuted for three years before one stone could be laid upon another. No man who could not swim was employed, and no landing from a boat was attempted except when convoyed by another boat. A surf boat manned with three lifeguards was kept constantly on duty while the workmen were on the ledge.

THE NANTUCKET LIGHTSHIP

It would be interesting to recount the stories of Cape Cod light, and of the lightships that mark the passage through the shoals off Cape Cod and through the sounds to Buzzards Bay. But whoever thinks of lightships, thinks first of Nantucket. Mr. George R. Putnam, chief of the Lighthouse Service, in his excellent book, "Lighthouses and Lightships of the United States," tells this story of the Nantucket lightship:

"On a voyage from Europe the weather had been such that the steamer had crossed the Atlantic without the officers having secured a single observation after leaving the Irish coast. A passenger came on deck on a misty evening and heard first faintly, and then louder, the blasts of a steam whistle at regular intervals of half a minute. Then through the thin fog a white light eclipsed every quarter of a minute, and there soon loomed out of the mist in the dusk a little vessel at anchor, rolling heavily in the swell, with a red hull, and *Nantucket* in large white letters on her side.

"The great liner swept by and on toward her port, for then it was that her master had definite knowledge that he was 200 miles east of New York harbor. This lightship, anchored on one of the most exposed stations in the world, has given this message to many thousands of captains and has been the first signpost of America to millions of passengers."

WITHSTANDING THE SIEGE GUNS OF THE SEA

The Nantucket lightship is anchored in 30 fathoms of water, 41 miles from the nearest land, Nantucket Island. She is 135 feet long, with full propelling power should she part her cables. She has a crew of 15, a submarine bell, and a wireless outfit.

When the sea brings up its siege guns and heavy artillery is the time of all others for the lightship to be on its station. It must wallow in the trough of the sea as best it can and ride out the storm at a standstill, lest some hapless master get caught in the drumfire of a terrific offensive.

Heading inward to New York, one might tell of the Fire Island Lightship and Ambrose Channel Lightship, the latter marking the beginning of the "run" to Europe and the end of the "run" to America.

Navesink light, built on the highland of the Jersey coast just below Sandy Hook, with its seven-ton bivalve revolving lens of the lightning

OVER THE TOP

Trained from childhood in sea-lore and surf-boating, there are no better boatmen in the world than a coast-guard crew. Launching or landing through a heavy surf requires superb skill, keen judgment, and much courage. The lack of any of these requisites spells almost certain disaster—a capsize if nothing worse.

type, has an estimated candle-power of 25,000,000, which makes it the most powerful light in America, if not, indeed, in the whole world. The curvature of the earth cuts off its direct rays at 22 miles, but its beam has been observed in the sky to a distance of more than 80 land miles.

There is many an inspiring tale of the sea connected with Barnegat light, Absecon light, the lights that proclaim the capes at the mouth of the Chesapeake, and others to the south.

Cape Hatteras light has the distinction of being the farthest distant from the main shore of all American lights, and it is also the tallest lighthouse in the country. Spiral-painted like old-fashioned stick-candy, it is visible for many miles amid the storm-tossed waters of the North Carolina coast.

Off Hatteras there is a lightship that for the high seas and dangerous storms it must ride out is a rival of Nantucket vessel. It is the Diamond Shoals lightship.

Beyond Hatteras there are numerous great lights along the Dixie shores, each with an interesting history, each with a long record of service performed in warning craft to steer clear of the fighting zone between the water and the land. They, as well as gas buoys, fog signals, and many other warnings and guides to shipping while in the battle area, invite attention.

THE COAST AND GEODETIC SURVEY, THE WAR CORRESPONDENT

But however attractive their story, they must stand aside while some account is given of the work of the Coast and Geodetic Survey, which is ever a neutral war correspondent at the battle-front chronicling every change in the battle-line and keeping its position up to the minute, lest shipping run upon a new bar without warning. With its ably-manned surveying vessels it journeys up and down the battle-front with an eye always out for shore changes, dangerous shoals, and such. Every skipper who sails the main may thus know where the mine-planters of the briny deep have been at work, and can steer clear of such fields.

WEARERS OF THE CROSS

In spite of all the warnings of light and bell and buoy; in spite of surveys and charts and mapped battle-fronts, there are still ships that will get into the danger zone and fall victims of the heavy artillery that sweeps the seas between deep water and the dry land. Shall they be left to perish with their crews and cargo? Not if the helping hand of Uncle Sam's coast guard can rescue them.

What tales these Red Cross men of the turbulent seas could tell! What hardships they endure! What perils they brave! To them the cry of distress in a storm-tossed ocean never goes up in vain. No bombardment of Neptune is ever so fierce that they will not dare it, no hope of a timely rescue is ever too slight to spur them on. The raging battle might as well be a blissful calm, for all its power to turn aside the life-savers from their stern duty. Aye, they may sink beneath the waves themselves, but to them even such a death is a lot infinitely preferred to life with an unheeded call from out the angry sea as a memory.

No one who has ever watched the sturdy life-savers man the lifeboat on an exposed shore and, against odds that seem insuperable, pull gallantly out into the tempest, can fail to appreciate either the stoutness of heart or the grandeur of purpose of these men. Where seemingly no boat could live, they manage to breast the storm, ride the billows, and reach the stranded vessel.

With a record of 1,500 instances of the rescues of lives and ships in a single year, it would seem invidious to single out one over another. A Sandy Hook station not long ago answered five calls in one day.

A Rhode Island station some time later saved 71 persons from the Portuguese brigantine *Est Thiago*. That vessel went ashore in a fog and was totally lost. A heavy surf was running when the brigantine struck, making the launching of a lifeboat to the rescue an exceedingly difficult and perilous undertaking. Moreover, the state of the sea, once a launching was

AN ANCIENT BATTLE-FIELD: THE SAND-DUNE RAMPARTS OF SOUTHERN FLORIDA

effected, was such that a boat could not run alongside the vessel. Her masts were gone, some of the planks of her port side were missing, her starboard rail was under water, and debris was thrashing around everything on board as well as over the side.

Both crew and passengers were in extreme jeopardy, and in great panic were calling for help. The commander of the lifeboat watched his chance and in the brief period between seas ran in under the flying jib-boom. Following his directions, those on board crawled out on the boom and dropped into the boat.

The rescuers did not risk stopping long under the boom—only long enough at a time to get three or four persons. The time limit of safety reached, they would scud away with all speed, to avoid being swamped or capsized by a breaking sea.

WORK OF THE
COAST GUARD CUTTERS

Nor can one overlook the coast guard cutter and its work. Under presidential orders, about a dozen of these vessels patrol assigned

A MASS ASSAULT

As the seas retreat after an unsuccessful attack, they carry along in their flight many prisoners, wrested from the land army, that are never to be set free or exchanged.

sections of the coastal waters from Eastport, Maine, to Cape Canaveral, Florida.

Provided with liberal supplies of food, water, and fuel, they put out to sea and cruise throughout the long winter months, ever vigilantly looking and listening for vessels in distress and for opportunities to be good friends in an hour of dire need.

One cutter covers the district between Great Egg Harbor, New Jersey, and Cape Hatteras.

The heavier the blows being struck by the sea the greater the need for these cutters to be on the watch. Ships aground, afire, in a collision, indeed any S.O.S. sends the cutters full steam ahead to the rescue. Now it may be a schooner, like the *Frederic A. Duggan*, in distress some 70 miles east of Nantucket Lightship, loaded with China clay, from Cardiff, half full of water, her provisions gone and her bottom so foul that only a gale could give her

AN OUTPOST OF PALMS STANDING GUARD AGAINST AN
ATTACK OF THE SEA ON THE SOUTHERN FLORIDA COAST

headway. Now it may be the *Bay State* on the rocks of Hollicom's Cove, Maine. Now the *Antilla* sends out an S.O.S. call that she is afire 120 miles east of Norfolk, and the *Onondaga* rushes to her rescue, and, finally, with other help, gets her into port, her cargo a total loss, but the ship saved. Or it may be the transport *Sumner*, which lost her bearings in a fog December 11, 1916, and went upon the rocks of Barnegat Shoals.

RED CROSS STATIONS

In viewing the Atlantic seaboard, one finds that the opposing forces in nature's unrelenting campaign have at least paused long enough to coöperate in the foundation of Red Cross stations in neutral territory. From Maine to Florida they have established, by mutual agreement, waters in which peace prevails—harbors where fleets may find haven while awaiting call.

Few stretches of coast line in the world have more of these stations. Maine with its Eastport, Belfast, Rockland, and Portland harbors; New Hampshire with its Portsmouth harbor; Massachusetts with the harbors of Newburyport, Gloucester, Salem, Lynn, Boston, New Bedford, and Fall River; Rhode Island with Newport, Providence, and Bristol harbors; and Connecticut with those of New London, New Haven, and Bridgeport, give New England many such bases of first importance.

Between the western nose of Long Island and the eastern projection of Staten Island, New York is given a harbor with an outlet that justifies its name of "The Narrows." Beyond lies the Upper Bay and above that the deep waters of the Lower Hudson and East River, giving the city more potential water front than any other municipality in the world. New Jersey has little to offer in harbors of first importance, except the one it shares with New York and those on Raritan Bay; but it joins with Delaware in forming Delaware Bay, with its ocean outlet for Philadelphia.

Further down the coast the land sank and invited the waters in through the Virginia capes to form harbors at Baltimore, Norfolk, Portsmouth, and Newport News. At Wilmington, N.C.; Charleston, S.C.; Savannah, Ga.; Jacksonville and Key West, Fla., are Red Cross stations of the first order, all directly or remotely built up by mutual consent of the warring elements, so that man, the innocent bystander, can seek safety when the front-line trenches become untenable for visitors.

THE SEA DOOMED TO DEFEAT

Such, briefly told, is the story of the great effort of the sea to bring the land under her dominion.

It is a warfare that has its lights and its shades, its tragedies and its joys. Furthermore, it is a warfare: with striking analogies to the great conflict of democracy against despotism, and just as surely as the upheavals that raised the Piedmont plains above the sea drove the ocean back and set the American continent firm and strong, so will democracy rise up in its power and successfully vanquish its foe, however subtle, however persistent, however relentless that foe may be.

AN IMPORTANT NEW GUIDE
FOR SHIPPING

Navassa Light, on a Barren Island in the West Indies, is the First Signal for the Panama Canal

By George R. Putnam

Commissioner of Lighthouses

LIGHTHOUSES and other sea marks are as necessary for the safety of traffic on the sea as are signal lights for the protection of railway travel.

It is interesting to note that there are waterways which are operated much like railways. Thus portions of the Detroit and St. Mary's rivers, which carry the enormous traffic between the Lakes, have practically been double-tracked by dredging and marking separate channels for up-bound and down-bound vessels, and in some narrow parts of this passage a block-system has recently been introduced, so that by means of semaphore signals a vessel is prevented from passing until the preceding vessel has gone a safe distance. Similar systems are in use on important canals.

In normal times the shipping of the North Atlantic is operated on a doubletrack plan, with distinct lanes agreed upon for east-bound and west-bound vessels, and these lanes are for safety shifted to the southward during the iceberg season.

New York has a sort of four-track entrance from the sea, and of the four channels leading to the Narrows, the great Ambrose Channel is reserved for express and high-class traffic, and sailing vessels and tows are not permitted to use it.

WHERE OCEAN TRAFFIC LINES CONVERGE

The great increase in the shipping interests of this country and the building of the Panama Canal have attracted attention to a large area which is poorly provided with safety signals for navigation. The Caribbean Sea, once known to fame mainly by the exploits of the early buccaneers, is now a region where ocean traffic converges from north, east, and south toward the Panama Canal.

The northwestern part of this sea is strewn with rocks, coral reefs, and submerged dangers, unlighted and unmarked, a constant menace to shipping from New Orleans and the Gulf, which must pass through lanes between the reefs, and from New York and the North Atlantic coast, which must go close to several of these dangers.

On one of these dangers, Navassa Island, 600 miles north of Colon, the first signal for the Panama Canal has recently been placed. On this barren and uninhabited rock the United States Lighthouse Service has built a lighthouse of unusual type.

The main route to the canal from our Atlantic seaboard is between Cuba and Haiti, through the Windward Passage, and Navassa Island, lying between Haiti and Jamaica, marks the southern approach to this passage, and is the first landfall for vessels from Panama crossing the Caribbean Sea. The importance of its position with respect to shipping to and from the canal caused the United States to undertake the building of a light station of the first class on this inhospitable rock.

NEW LIGHT SWEEPS AN AREA AS LARGE AS DELAWARE

After many difficulties of construction, due to the inaccessibility and character of the island, on October 21, 1917, the light was first shown from the new concrete tower. Every night since then two beams of 47,000 candlepower have swept around the horizon each 30 seconds with clocklike regularity. Instead of a dark rock, which had loomed in the night in this passage, threatening mariners since the days of the early voyagers, these great rays now flash out friendly guidance to the seamen of all countries, regardless of nationality; the beams of this light have been seen 29 sea miles away, reaching nearly to the Haitian coast, and they sweep a sea area of about 2,200 square statute miles, as large as the State of Delaware.

Navassa light, on this rock in the center of one of the principal international sea passages and 500 miles from the American coast, is the most important lighthouse built by the United States in the last quarter century.

A TOWER TO WITHSTAND HURRICANES AND EARTHQUAKES

Navassa Island has the outline of an oyster shell and is slightly more than a mile in area. As the island rises fairly abruptly on all sides, forming a roughly flat tableland about 200 feet above the sea, it was necessary to build a tower 150 feet in height, in order that the light might "see over" the edge of the plateau and not be obscured to vessels in the vicinity of the island, unless close under the cliffs. The tower was placed on the highest part, bringing the light 395 feet above the sea.

The lighthouse tower was designed to withstand West Indian hurricanes as well as earthquakes, and the lower sections have massive proportions, the base being 25 feet in diameter, with walls over 6 feet thick. It is built of reinforced concrete, one of the tallest towers yet constructed by this method; it is of simple and dignified design, bell-shaped at the base, and above that a simple cylinder to the watch-room gallery. The use of this structural material has resulted in a much more slender outline than has been necessary in masonry lighthouses.

Almost everything required for this work had to be brought from a distance; the skilled employees were sent from the United States,

THE BEGINNING OF THE CONSTRUCTION OF THE TALL LIGHTHOUSE,
SHOWING THE STEEL REINFORCEMENT IN PLACE FOR THE FOUNDATION
AND BASE OF THE TOWER

The steel skeleton, around which the concrete of the tower was poured, consists of 40 vertical steel bars, band-
ed by a spiral of round steel bars, with loops one foot apart, wired to each vertical bar.

together with all special supplies and equipment; the laborers came from Cuba and
Jamaica, and it was even necessary to bring
from Jamaica all the sand and most of the water
used in construction.

The nearest ports were Guantanamo,
Cuba, 90 miles, and Kingston, Jamaica, 110
miles distant. No good landing exists on the
island, so that the little schooner that was used
to bring supplies and men had to be moored
under the rocky cliffs, when weather favored,

and the cargo hoisted onto the shelf above; this
small craft had narrow escapes from hurricanes,
and there were many days when it was impossible to land.

On one occasion, after being damaged in a
storm, the schooner with her load of supplies put
back to Jamaica, and there was apprehension as
to the food on Navassa, but this reassuring
report was received: "The last flour was used for
making bread on Friday. There were sufficient
rations on hand to last through Sunday, and with

NAVASSA ISLAND LIGHT STATION, WEST INDIES:
SCHOONER IN LULU BAY UNLOADING SAND

A little nook called Lulu Bay, with the schooner moored to the cliff; this is the only landing place available on Navassa Island. All the supplies and material for the lighthouse construction, as well as the workmen, were brought to the island by this little schooner, which was the only means of transportation for the year and nine months that the work was in progress.

NAVASSA LIGHTHOUSE

Built by the United States Lighthouse Service, of reinforced concrete, on an uninhabited island in the West Indies. The concrete tower is 150 feet in height. The dwelling for the keepers is shown to the right.

goats, wild pigeons, fish, etc., together with a pig and a number of chickens which are kept here, we were in no serious predicament."

An unusual feature in lighthouse building, a radio equipment, much facilitated construction.

Men quickly tired of the monotonous life. On account of climate and difficulty of transportation, very little fresh food was available, and the workmen persistently grumbled. The excessive heat soon diminished their efficiency. The transportation of materials from the landing place to the site was a most burdensome task, as this had to be done largely by men shoving the loaded cars on the work railway.

ISLAND RESEMBLES
A PETRIFIED SPONGE

Navassa is one of the strangest pieces of territory owned by the United States. It is a remarkable formation of volcanic limestone, completely riddled with holes and pockets, some of great depth and having no visible bottom. These holes are so numerous that one can walk only with great difficulty.

There is a total absence of water, and no watercourses or lakes, as rain is immediately absorbed by the cavities. The whole island has the appearance of a great petrified sponge. There is a growth of stunted trees and underbrush on the high plateau, and the island has some animal life, wild goats and wild cats, doubtless descended from those brought here when the island was occupied, and numerous seabirds and land-crabs.

UNITED STATES'
TITLE TO ISLAND RESTS
ON MURDER-TRIAL DECISION

It is a curious fact that the title of the United States to Navassa Island rests on the deci-

sion in a murder trial. Although uninhabited and long abandoned at the time the lighthouse work was undertaken, Navassa was for some years actively occupied. The pockets and surface of the island contained a large deposit of a phosphate earth and guano.

Under the guano act of 1856, one Peter Duncan presented a memorial to the Secretary of State stating "that on the first day of July, in the year of 1857, he did discover a deposit of guano on an island or key in the Caribbean Sea not occupied by the citizens of any other government, and that he did take peaceable possession of and occupy said island or key of Navassa in the name of the United States." These deposits were worked by a company for a number of years, up to 1898, and the ruins indicate an elaborate plant for this purpose.

In 1889 about 150 men were employed on the island, and on September 14 of that year a riot occurred, in which the superintendent and several of his assistants were killed. The frigate *Kearsarge* took the murderers off the island and they were tried in Baltimore.

The defense set up the plea that the island was not an American possession and that the court had no jurisdiction, but the Supreme Court denied this plea and the murderers were executed.

A concrete dwelling, in the Spanish style, with a large open patio in the center, furnishes comfortable quarters for the families of the three keepers who carefully watch this, one of the loneliest of the sea signals of this country. They see many a passing ship, but can expect supplies and mail only when the supply steamer visits the island, a few times a year.

The matter of marking other dangerous reefs of the Caribbean Sea for the protection of the increased shipping is now receiving special consideration.

FURTHER READING

There are a number of excellent books about these structures. See especially the six volumes written by Bruce Roberts and Ray Jones between 1993–1996. Cheryl Shelton-Roberts and Bruce Roberts, *Lighthouse Families* (1997), deals with the daily life of American families who live in lighthouses. See also Amy Handy, *The Lighthouse* (1997), Elinore De Wire, *Guardians of the Lights: Stories of Us Lighthouse Keepers* (1998), and John Grant and Ray Jones, *Legendary Lighthouses* (1998).

INDEX

CONTRIBUTORS

General Editor FRED L. ISRAEL is an award-winning historian. He received the Scribe's Award from the American Bar Association for his work on the Chelsea House series *The Justices of the United States Supreme Court*. A specialist in American history, he was general editor for Chelsea's *1897 Sears Roebuck Catalog*. Dr. Israel has also worked in association with Arthur M. Schlesinger, jr. on many projects, including *The History of the U.S. Presidential Elections* and *The History of U.S. Political Parties*. He is senior consulting editor on the Chelsea House series *Looking into the Past: People, Places, and Customs*, which examines past traditions, customs, and cultures of various nations.

Senior Consulting Editor ARTHUR M. SCHLESINGER, JR. is the pre-eminent American historian of our time. He won the Pulitzer Prize for his book *The Age of Jackson* (1945), and again for *A Thousand Days* (1965). This chronicle of the Kennedy Administration also won a National Book Award. He has written many other books, including a multi-volume series, *The Age of Roosevelt*. Professor Schlesinger is the Albert Schweitzer Professor of the Humanities at the City University of New York, and has been involved in several other Chelsea House projects, including the *American Statesmen* series of biographies on the most prominent figures of early American history.